MW00784928

My Kingdom
Is in
Your Heart

Letters to the Duchess of Orléans
and
Meditations on Christian Life

Mother Mectilde de Bar

My Kingdom
Is in
Your Heart

⊕

Letters to the Duchess of Orléans
and
Meditations on Christian Life

FOREWORD BY
Abbot Xavier Perrin, OSB

✿ Angelico Press

First published in English
by Angelico Press 2023
© Angelico Press 2023
Foreword by Abbot Xavier Perrin, OSB
Translated by an Oblate
of Silverstream Priory
All rights reserved

For information, address:
Angelico Press
169 Monitor St.
Brooklyn, NY 11222
www.angelicopress.com

978-1-62138-920-0 (pbk)
978-1-62138-921-7 (cloth)

Cover design: Julian Kwasniewski

CONTENTS

Foreword

A great lady in a great century

In seventeenth-century France, Mectilde de Bar (1614–1698), a woman of exceptional energy, considerable gifts, rich experience and total commitment to God, founded a new Benedictine Congregation, with a special dedication to the perpetual adoration of the Blessed Sacrament. She addressed the texts collected and translated here to different correspondents over a long period of time. If the first part of the book draws on a single source, the letters she wrote to Marguerite de Lorraine, Duchess of Orléans (1615–1672), the texts of the second part have been gathered from a series of sources and circulated within the Congregation for centuries before they began to reach a wider public only recently, first in the original language and now in translation.

We cannot fully appreciate all these usually short texts out of the context of the veneration with which they were handed on from one generation of nuns to another over centuries. Pious eyes have meditated on these texts long before us. Lives have been inspired by them. Sinners have been helped in their struggles. Saintly souls have been confirmed in their dedication to God. The disadvantage of a collection of texts from different dates and addressed to different people, when one would perhaps prefer a more developed and ordered treatise, is amply counterbalanced by the profound unity of vision which emanates from their author. In this book, *someone* is speaking to us. We do not meet with ideas but with a person who is sharing with us her profound intimacy with God.

Mectilde's style is simple, light and luminous. Her mind is precise and clear. She goes right to the point which she wishes to make; she is direct, without violence. One can feel a very peaceful soul, deeply rooted in God. Her tone is gentle, even when she is demanding. Her touch is always light and elegant. She has an immense respect for

1

each soul. She is maternal without being too affective, strong without any stiffness. Even when she uses the rather extreme vocabulary of her time, she does it in a manner which remains balanced, sound and humble. For the *Grand Siècle* had a high conception of God's grandeur and human littleness—God alone is great; man is nothingness—as well as of the sacrificial dimensions of the Incarnation: Christ becomes a victim, to Whom in return all has to be immolated.

The nothingness of man

The Renaissance had exalted man's presence at the center of the universe to the point of leading him to forget that he had been created and did not create himself. The religious reaction against this dangerous exaltation—which can still be recognized nowadays in the model of the "self-made man"—was to insist on man's humble condition. Man is a creature and a sinner, incapable by himself of any greatness. But God loved him and redeemed him in Jesus Christ. The Blood of Jesus Christ poured out on the Cross out of love is the price He paid for every soul.

Mectilde stands with what has been called "augustinianism," a theological and anthropological vision inherited from St Augustine and his followers, and largely shared in her time. However, whereas others, such as Calvinists or Jansenists, develop a very pessimistic vision of the human condition and of salvation, she belongs to a current of thought which, in the wake of St Francis de Sales (1567–1622) and Cardinal Pierre de Bérulle (1575–1629), holds together man's humility and God's mercy, thus seeing all things in the positive light of God's love and generosity. She draws souls into a climate of trust and humble confidence. For God "wants you to be completely His; but in love and through the path of love, and not through sadness and fear, which is the ruin of pure love" (*n.* 1549, 64). She shows the way to a peace she herself has obviously reached.

The first step towards such a peace, which we often need to repeat, consists in consenting to one's humble condition which, using the vocabulary common to her time, she describes as "nothingness." You are nothing of yourself. All that you are, all the good you do come from God. "God is everything and the creature is

2

nothing. God is of Himself, God is through Himself, God is for himself. All creatures have their existence in God in such a way that if He withdrew His support for one moment, all creatures would be reduced to nothing; these are dogmas of faith which we are required to believe" (*n.* 1694, 163). Any other view of yourself can only come from pride. Humility is this truth about who you really are: "Humility does not consist of having humble thoughts but in bearing the weight of the truth, which is the abyss of our extreme misery, when it pleases God to make us feel it" (*n.* 1700, LP, 160). For Mectilde, this truth has an essential practical dimension. We correspond to this truth when we "reduce ourselves to nothing"—our projects, our ideas, our desires and wills—so as to leave space for God in our lives.

God's indwelling presence

For if we discover the reality of our created being, we shall also realize the marvel of our Baptism. In this great sacrament, God purifies us from sin, but above all, He establishes His dwelling in our souls. Our nothingness is inhabited. The creature, bathed in God's grace, becomes the temple of the Holy Trinity. The Augustinian lesson of interiority is embraced by Mectilde who never tires of inviting us to discover the great God who dwells in us. Spiritual life is about knowing that you are nothing, believing that God lives in you, and, out of love for Him, adoring Him and consenting to do His will in all things.

To this end, she preaches the classical exercises of silence and solitude, recollection and prayer. You do not need hours of contemplative prayers, though. She is very insistent that a simple "quarter of an hour" can be a most efficacious means of sanctification for people from all walks of life. In silent solitude, the disciple begins with making an act of faith: "I believe that You are what You are, and I believe myself to be a pure nothing in your holy Presence." Then, keeping humble and quiet, the soul is invited to "restrain the acts of [the] mind so as to feel only the delicate touches of the Holy Spirit," for it is about "doing on earth what we hope to do for all eternity": "love, adore, and possess within ourselves the same God who is the glory and the felicity of the blessed" (*n.* 215, 76). Interiority is not an end in itself (for we are nothing). It has to lead to God, who is in us and above us at the same time, and into whom the soul is invited to "sink": "Let yourself sink into this adorable All" (ibid.).

What might at first sight look like a "method," or even a "trick," reveals itself as a *way* and a spiritual path on which one has to persevere in faith, in hope and in love. The spiritual mistress is not speaking to the intellect once for all, but accompanying with great mercy and hope the slow progress of souls. She supports them with her gentle, balanced and very patient guidance. Her maternal presence is what makes this book so real, and so helpful. Her spiritual motherhood is made accessible to many.

Mystagogy

Being a daughter of St Benedict, Mectilde unsurprisingly pays great attention to the liturgy. The liturgical background of all that she says can be felt everywhere. More especially, the liturgical year, with the celebrations of Our Lord, Our Lady and the Saints, provides her with the opportunity to show how the life of the soul can partake in the mysteries which the Church celebrates. The present edition aptly chooses to arrange many texts according to a liturgical pattern and we can be grateful for this judicious decision. For the spiritual mother who is Mectilde cannot be separated from Mother Church herself who, in the celebrations of the liturgical seasons, teaches her children the rules of the life in the Spirit. Attentiveness to the moods and attitudes which a given liturgical context suggests is key to learning how to follow the indications of the Spirit. It also provides the soul with an opportunity to broaden her views beyond her own concerns and efforts and to situate these in the context of an ecclesial journey.

Through the Sacraments and the liturgy as a whole, the Church forms in the soul the dispositions that were in Christ Jesus. Or, to put it even more precisely, Christ Himself is living out His whole mystery in the mysteries of the Church and inviting the soul to take part in it. Mectilde has a vivid awareness that He dies on the altar and that we, too, die with Him in order to enter the fullness of life of the resurrection. This is another dimension—Christological—of being "reduced to nothing": the *kenosis* of the Son in His Incarnation and on the Cross is represented in the sacrifice of the altar so that it can be offered as the perfect redemptive sacrifice by the Church and fulfilled in the souls of believers. Mectilde's soul is powerfully drawn in this direction. She thirsts for a perfect identification with Christ in His Paschal Mystery. Her whole life is placed under the sign of Christ who, according to the *Letter to the Philippians*, made Himself obedient unto death on the cross. She is not tempted by any voluntaristic imitation of a divine example; Pelagianism is not for her. She relies on Christ and His Spirit; she draws her strength and the dynamism of her spiritual life from Them alone and she teaches her disciples to do the same. Hence her tone, which is always more suggestive and inviting than prescriptive or authoritarian. There is no stiffness in her soul, but only a remarkable suppleness to the impulse of the Spirit leading her into Christ's salvific obedience.

It would be a total error to consider her as someone whose spiritual life consist mainly in devotions, even the most pious and commendable ones. She belongs fully to the current of authentic Benedictine spirituality which is essentially mystagogical. The mysteries of our salvation in Christ are represented in the actions of the liturgy which God Himself renders effective and transformative of the life of believers. She does not lead you to any secondary river, but to the main current of divine life imparted through the sacramental actions of the Church. She has found the source of divine love and leads others to find it in their turn. Hence her surety and her peace; her clarity and her humility; her exigencies and her patience.

In the Heart of Jesus

The story of the rediscovery of the Sacred Heart of Jesus as symbol of divine love in the seventeenth century, notably through the teaching of St Jean Eudes (1601–1680) and the apparitions of Our Lord to St Marguerite Marie Alacoque (1647–1690), is well known. For Mectilde, the Sacred Heart of Jesus, burning with divine love, "is in reality the true and essential repose" (*n.* 3097, LO, 48). She writes that it is "the blessed center of [one's] soul" (ibid.). Mectilde is, or longs to be (but is it not nearly the same?), hidden in the Sacred Heart of Jesus, and this is also where she sees her sisters or correspondents. She invites them to remain in it as much as they can; this is also the way she suggests they can deal with their sufferings and crosses.

She invites the Duchesse of Orléans, who meets with great opposition and contradictions, to keep her peace: "Do not lose your repose, do not alter your peace. God is... He is in you, He is with you, He is for you... If you dwell in Him, He will dwell in you" (*n.* 708, 72). She must learn to see all her sufferings, all her crosses, as allowed by God, ordained by His Providence, "being attached only to the good pleasure of God, so that the troubles of life do not disturb the tranquility of your heart" (ibid.). This is founded on faith, a faith able to "go straight to God" (ibid.). There is a special peace in understanding that God is at work in all the circumstances of one's life. He wills the good of the soul and ordains all things to this end. It is therefore enough for the soul to "see [one]self as a little ball of wax in the hand of God, to be formed according to His pleasure" (*n.* 2933, 76).

It should be noted here that it is precisely in the context of dealing with sufferings that Mectilde gives the most detailed presentation of the "little quarter of an hour." This must therefore not be understood just as a practice of devotion for those benefiting from favorable circumstances. It is by touching one's nothingness, adhering to God's loving presence and conforming oneself to His will, that a soul keeps its peace and deepens its love for God. We are far from any Christian stoicism. Sufferings are not dealt with by an effort of detachment and voluntary resignation, but by strengthening the contact with God through genuine humility, strong faith, and ardent charity. Mectilde's advice is immediately theological, or even one could say, mystical. It consists in embracing the mystery of God, for "we must be entirely God's" as an answer to "a God so close to us, and in a manner so beyond words that it seems that He has nothing to do except give Himself completely to us and fill us with His graces" (*n.* 3123, 80).

The sacrament of love
Mectilde finds in the Holy Eucharist a perfect revelation of God's love. "The divine Eucharist is matter for a greater rapture [than the

Incarnation], since in it we adore a God so smitten with love for His poor creature that He finds the means to dwell with her until the end of the ages and to produce every day the fruits of His ineffable mysteries" (*n.* 1123, 52). God "reduces Himself to nothing" under the Species in order "to enter our hearts". He becomes a victim of His love for us on the altar. This seems to be the highest revelation of His love. To communicate is indeed to receive God in ourselves. His love urges us to welcome Him in faith: "enter into him through a profound surrender of your entire self. This is the effect of *Pascha*, which is the passage of Jesus, so that Jesus may live in you and so that your soul may be entirely lost in Him" (ibid.).

The Sisters of the Congregation she founded understand themselves as "victims of His divine Sacrament" (*n.* 388, 110). They are indeed wounded by the revelation of divine love in the Eucharist and commit themselves in return to a life of adoration. They become Christ's victims as He became theirs in the manger (*n.* 2629, 25), for "the soul become nothing abides in God, becoming one spirit with Him" (ibid.). They "adore Him on His Eucharistic throne, where love will immolate Him for you and will draw you into His sacrifice, to be made one and the same victim with Him" (*n.* 1145, 33). "I desire for you […] to be a pure victim for the divine love" (*n.* 1763, 61). For "it is the joy and the delight of the saints to suffer and die for God, and to see themselves become a victim united to the sacrifice of Jesus Christ" (*n.* 2439, 55).

A great Benedictine master

In the "school of love" initiated by St Benedict (480–547), Mectilde de Bar shines out as a great master. She invites souls to open themselves to divine love with a humility, a power, even a charm that are fully Benedictine. She has the balance and the broadness of the Benedictine school. She ranks among these great abbesses who, in a century of holiness and fervor, were true lights of the Benedictine Order.[1] She provides us with what we always need: a simple and practical invitation to believe in the love God has for us. This

1. See my *In the School of St Benedict: Benedictine Spirituality for Every Christian* (Leominster: Gracewing, 2022), especially Chapter 2.

woman was seized by divine love and had no other aim than helping us, too, to realize with St John: "See what kind of love the Father has given to us, that we should be called children of God; and so we are" (1 Jn 3:1).

ABBOT XAVIER PERRIN OSB
Quarr Abbey, August 2022

Note on Sources

Part I of this volume translates pages 19–98 from the *Lettres Inédites* compiled by the Benedictines of the Blessed Sacrament of Rouen and published by them in 1976. All of the selections are translated here, but somewhat reorganized into thematic groups. Part II is a translation of *Adorer et adhérer* (*To Adore and to Adhere*), also compiled by the Benedictines of the Blessed Sacrament of Rouen, and published by Éditions du Cerf, 1994. In a few instances, Part II reproduces sentences that are also translated in Part I.

Psalms are cited according to their Vulgate numbering.

Part I

Letters to the Duchess of Orléans

MARGVERITE DE LORRAINE, DVC[HE]SSE D'ORLEANS deuxiesme Fille de Fr-
ançois Comte de Vaudemont et de Christine de Salm. Son Altesse Royalle Gaston de France Duc
d'Orleans de Chartres et de Valois, contracta alliance auec ceste Illustre et Vertueise Princesse l'an 1632 en qu-
oy sa constance et sa generosité ont fait voir un exemple qui sera à iamais admiré de la posterité; pour auoir
cueilly, sous le Regne du feu Roy Louis le Iuste son frere, ceste fleur au milieu de plusieurs espines. Aussy
Dieu a comblé ce Mariage de bonheur, par vne lignée qui a fait renouueller en la personne du ieune Duc
de Valois, la branche d'Orleans seconde tige de plusieurs Roys et Princes du Sang de la Maison de France.
Ce ieune Prince mourut au Palais D'orleans le 10. Aoust 1652. aagé de 2 ans.

Marguerite of Lorraine
by the translator

Marguerite of Lorraine (July 22, 1615–April 13, 1672) was the daughter of Francis II, Duke of Lorraine, and Countess Christina of Salm. One of six children, she grew up in Nancy, the capital of her father's duchy.[1] After losing her mother in 1627, Marguerite was raised and educated by her aunt, Catherine of Lorraine, the Abbess of Remiremont. Catherine was passionate about the Counter-Reformation program of the Church and succeeded in starting a new Benedictine congregation following the Strict Observance. She was also foundress of the Benedictine convent of Our Lady of Consolation in Nancy. Catherine's spiritual character had a profound formative effect on her niece.

In January 1632, Marguerite secretly wed Gaston, Duke of Orléans, younger brother of Louis XIII of France and, at that time, heir presumptive. As Gaston had married in secret, in defiance of the King, Louis XIII declared their marriage null when the fact became known. Gaston refused to accept the annulment of the marriage, but did little to be reunited with his wife. During this period, Marguerite was "begging her bread" as she wrote to her brother, the Duke of Lorraine, who also gave her scant aid. Despite all this, she maintained her affection for Gaston and her family. The letters she wrote to Gaston reveal her suffering and her sincere love:

> I complain of my misfortune rather than complaining of you, for you will easily see, with everyone else, that I am the most unhappy of women… For so many years I have been in the most difficult state that ever was, not knowing whom I could turn to, whom to call on, except God and my tears. What grieves me most is that

1. The Duchy of Lorraine or Lothringen was founded in 959 and came under Polish rule in 1737; it passed to the French crown in 1766.

this life [you are living] is detrimental to your honor…, for finally, I love you and honor you with all my heart; I know also that you love me; surely, you have cause to. Therefore, make it known… so that I may be with you soon, to make a life for myself in accordance with God's will and which is edifying to the world. (March 19, 1638)

Marguerite led an exemplary life; her constancy finally overcame both the royal opposition and the spousal passivity it encountered. In 1643, on his deathbed, Louis XIII finally allowed her to come to France and gave his consent to the marriage. He declared he was "persuaded to do so, by the very special esteem we have had for the merit and piety of our sister-in-law."[2]

Having finally settled in the Palais de Luxembourg, Marguerite and Gaston had five children, two of whom died in infancy. Marguerite endured many difficulties: an unreliable husband, a troublesome stepdaughter, constant moving from one place to another, civil strife both in France and Lorraine, toxic intrigues at the court, financial worries, physical ailments. Despite all this, she maintained her deep faith. Ultimately she converted Gaston as well. He took as his confessor Armand-Jean Bouthillier de Rancé, the famous reforming Cistercian.

It is not known exactly under what circumstances Marguerite became acquainted with Mother Mectilde, but since both were refugees from Lorraine, living near each other in Paris, it was a natural connection. The Duchess aided the new Benedictine institute both financially and with her connections in Rome and in the court. She worked for the aggregation of the monastery under her influence, Our Lady of Consolation in Nancy, to Mother Mectilde's new Benedictine institute.

Marguerite also benefited as a frequent visitor to the convent for adoration and spiritual counsel. Between visits, the Prioress and the Duchess exchanged letters. The Prioress, whose letters are published here, wrote as "Novice Mistress" to the Duchess, her "Novice." Written in the grand manner of the "great century," the letters exhibit

---

2. Pierre Marot, Introduction to the Letters to the Duchess, in *Lettres Inédites* (Rouen: Benedictines of the Blessed Sacrament, 1976), 11.

both liberty of expression and the courtly deference of the period. While there are details that apply to the period and particular troubles Marguerite faced, the letters are most valuable for showcasing Mother Mectilde's profound insights: admirable meditations on liturgical feasts, practical prayer advice, and spiritual counsel of perennial value.

Despite her many health problems, Marguerite after her husband's death entertained the idea of giving up everything and devoting her life solely to God, living as a lay sister in a monastery of the Benedictines of the Blessed Sacrament. While Mectilde was in favor of this project, she continually encouraged the Duchess to mature into a pure renunciation, which is ultimately an interior disposition: "Act before God as if everything was lost for you, so that from now on you can say to Him: 'I am content with You alone. My kingdom is in Your Heart and Yours is in mine.'"

The Duchess never was able to enter the convent as she wished, but departed for the heavenly kingdom in 1672. She was buried at the Basilica of Saint Denis. Her tomb was destroyed during the French Revolution.

Advent

On the desires of Jesus: For the holy season of Advent

You have too much kindness and concern for my health. It is so great that I wish that your health was whole and perfect also, and I beg you most humbly to not trouble yourself about so trivial a matter. I am eating eggs and I have taken some rich broth out of obedience to you and to please our Mother Sub-prioress who stands strong as a fortress, since you are taking her side.

I hoped to have the honor of seeing you yesterday so that we could converse and so that I could gently waken you. Madam, now is the time of desires. The Church is completely filled with them and she shows it through the Divine Office. Let us unite ourselves to her and cry out with the just: *Rorate caeli desuper et nubes pluant justum.*[1] Let us rejoice at the coming of the eternal Word clothed in our flesh; let us prepare ourselves to welcome Him and to give Him absolute power over us. Since He comes to reign in us, and His reign ought to have no end or limit, we must give Him none. Oh, what happiness to be the subject of a King who gives His life for His subjects and who makes them partakers of His glory![2] Furthermore, He makes us His children and communicates to us His holy dispositions, merits, perfections, mysteries, and above all, His divine life, and so we are the more required to imitate it. Oh, what gifts and favors! A soul would be very hard to please who refused them and did not want to abandon herself to Him. Let us give Him all in exchange for all. Blessed is the soul who possesses its adorable Jesus and seeks only to please Him! Love, Madam, love, this is the sweetest and easiest and also the most consistent with His grace in you.

---

1. Is 45:8. Drop down ye heavens from above and let the clouds rain down the Just One.
2. 1 Pt 5:1.

We will say more when we have the honor of seeing you.

I take great joy in the good hope you are giving me. I have seen the clergyman whom you know. Nothing must be neglected. I should see him tomorrow. I will write to you about it.

I embrace your feet with profound respect.

n. 3021

Disposition for Advent

You give me news which I cherish with all my heart, and from the depths of my soul I give thanks to God that He has preserved your health. You are exceedingly kind to a creature who cannot deserve it and who would wish to be at your feet for the rest of her life, to sacrifice myself along with you, Madam, to the One who is immolated every day on the altar for us to His Father. I am eager to give myself to Jesus in the most perfect manner, as He desires it from me.

It seems to me that we have almost no time and must not delay any longer. Time goes on and eternity approaches. If I followed my own feelings, I would flee to the desert, so as not to be in the world any longer. But [in this] I would not be heeding the primary business, which is to go out of myself in order to give life to Jesus.

Madam, grant me a small share in your holy prayers, and make the act of charity you know, to honor the birth of the Holy Child Jesus in your most dear and kind heart. This is the very humble prayer of the one who is more deeply yours than she can say.

n. 3093

Christmas

On the Nativity of Our Lord

I just received the enclosed items which I am sending you shortly, wishing you good day, and asking for news of your health. I hope it is perfect, so that your soul may rise more easily to God. Since that is your whole occupation now, I wish that it may be so continually and entreat you not to defer any longer being completely His. You have a good Novice Master who will guide you in this, incomparably better than a Novice Mistress [and you will find everything in him].[1] It is worth a good deal when someone can say, "*Ego te...*"[2] The Novice Mistress cannot say it. But since your humility desires this, she will take the liberty to arouse your soul, from time to time, to proceed always more resolutely towards its center.

This holy season is wonderful for making us advance. The mysteries of Our Lord's childhood are so full of sweetness and love that the souls who focus on them become entirely inebriated with them. Experience the sweetness of a God reduced to nothing[3] in the virginal womb of His blessed Mother. Embrace His feet and do not leave them. Enter into the dispositions of His most Sacred Heart: into the deepest abasement before this infinite greatness, over-

---

1. A manuscript variant.
2. *Ego te absolvo...* I absolve you.
3. Strictly speaking, the term *anéanti* should be translated as annihilated, destroyed, and *anéantissement* as annihilation, destruction. However, in this spiritual context it means *kenosis* or exinanition—a death to self producing the most profound humility. In order to avoid misunderstanding it has been translated throughout as reduced or brought to nothing, with Psalm 73:22 in mind. See also *The "Breviary of Fire": Letters by Mother Mectilde of the Blessed Sacrament, Chosen and Arranged by the Countess of Châteauvieux*, trans. an Oblate of Silverstream Priory (Brooklyn, NY: Angelico Press, 2021), xxiii–xxviii.

whelmed and as if lost, before the nothingness and weakness of human nature; in gratitude for His love which reduced Him to that condition, to relieve our misery and open paradise for us; the tenderness and love of a goodness which forgets itself in order to fill us with graces. Do not distance yourself from His holy Presence. Try to enter into it when you leave your duties, when, for the sake of necessary business, you have been obliged to leave it. Speak with that noble Mother, and entreat her to cause you to enter into the dispositions you must have to share in the graces which the renewal of the divine mystery should produce in your soul. Believe that the more you are God's the more blessing you will have in your affairs and the more contentment and joy in your heart.

Start, and never stop, receiving Communion on all Saturdays and feasts. I will never have any consolation unless I see your soul possessing this holy practice, whatever favor you show me by honoring me with your friendship. I ask it of you with as much earnestness as someone ambitious for the highest good fortune. And I dare to say that I am asking it on behalf of my God who desires this of you. He desires to come to you and nevertheless you do not receive Him. You have many small weaknesses that will only be eradicated by availing yourself of this Eucharistic bread. Why deprive your soul of an infinite good? Listen to the voice of this adorable Savior who calls from your heart's depths: *"Aperi, aperi mihi, soror mea, sponsa mea."* "Open to Me, open your heart to Me, My sister, My bride, My beloved, that I may make My eternal dwelling in it and take My rest in you." He wants to be united to you, to make you entirely one with Himself. Do not refuse what the angels consider themselves infinitely blessed and unworthy to receive. Surely, if you do not listen to this divine voice I will be a thousand times more aggrieved than if I was condemned to death. I see the moments passing, the weeks and months, and that, because of I do not know what temptation, you are delaying your eternal happiness. I beg you not to go on any longer like this, for fear that, when you desire to receive Communion, you no longer can: and in the meanwhile you are depriving your soul of the divine life.

Pardon, Madam, for I confess my boldness to you. However, I do not promise that I will correct myself, since I have too much fond-

20

ness for your soul. It is too dear and too precious to me not to wish passionately for you the greatest good that your soul could ever have.

n. 1580

On the Holy Child Jesus (1)

Will we have the favor of being consoled with your most honored presence? If I could break the chains that keep me in my dear prison,[4] I would not delay in coming to your feet to be reassured about your health and ask you for the news of this Child-God, whom we can call the newborn King. He is in a palace where all the decoration to be found is an extreme poverty: a cradle lined with hay, adorned with cobwebs, with a complete abandonment by all creatures. Jesus, Mary and Joseph are alone in the stable, in complete forgetfulness of the whole world, after the visit of the shepherds, and in an amazing solitude. The infant Jesus, in His captivity and His silence, offers Himself to the Father as a victim, to restore His glory and to reconcile mankind with His Father; Mary, His precious Mother, enters into the dispositions of her dear Son, and makes herself a single offering with Him, through an incomprehensible love and transformation; in a mysterious silence Joseph adores and contemplates what the human mind cannot understand.

Three things are shared by these holy persons, Jesus, Mary and Joseph: silence, prayer, and sacrifice. And these three things are necessary if we would imitate their dispositions and be pleasing to them. Ask for these for me, even as I will do for you with all my heart. I must finish now as it is time for high Mass.

n. 47

On the Holy Child Jesus (2)

I have not roused your dear person, because I have not thought you to be asleep. The desire to belong to God and to love Him seemed to me many times to quicken your heart. The heart wishes to rise above itself to remain in God; but the weight of human misery does not allow it to enjoy this happiness in this life without intermission. We

---

4. The cloister.

must suffer the length of our exile in patience. It will be easier for us to bear this if we consider the Eternal Word under the image of our flesh, who comes today to be our companion in the pilgrimage.

He came to the world and the world did not receive Him. He came to His own and they did not recognize Him. Here is Jesus on earth, then, like a stranger; He has no place to dwell or to rest His head. It is His love for us which reduced Him to this poverty. My God, how great this love is—to bring Jesus to nothingness! Among His subjects, He is like a slave, and all His actions are simply the marvelous inventions of His love, for the sake of drawing us to Himself; to win our hearts and give us the freedom to converse with Him, and no longer doubt His kindness toward us; and so that we no longer cling to thoughts of mistrust and fear which trouble and disturb our minds. The Eternal Father gave His Son to the Holy Virgin, and that blessed Mother gave Him to us today. Let us rejoice in such a gift, which contains everything. In Him let us find everything we need. We will receive help from Him if we try to enter into His new life. But what is that life? It is sacrifice, death, becoming nothing. He was no sooner on the straw than He became the victim of the divine justice and holiness. All His grandeurs are buried in lowliness and His powers in powerlessness.

n. 1040

On the Holy Child Jesus (3)

Madam, although your kindness has done me the favor of sending word that your illness was of no consequence, I could not help being quite worried and I have redoubled prayers, asking God more fervently than ever to preserve you. We are all going to Communion for this intention and for all your spiritual and temporal needs. If Our Lord deigns to listen to my sighing, He will fill you with the grace and understanding of the sacred mystery which we are worshipping today. If this Child God appears in the depths of your heart, His presence will make you rejoice and His love will strengthen you.

There is nothing sweeter than to love and to know Jesus; the prophet assures us of this.[5] Love, love this adorable Savior who

5. Ps 118:103; Ps 18:10.

22

loves you so tenderly and who applies His merits and everything that He is in Himself to you. Delight in Him and find in His fullness everything you lack. Make use of His virtues and love to make up for everything [you lack], and rest in His kindness with childlike trust. You will experience that your hope will not be in vain or your trust misplaced. Take heart, therefore, Madam, and seek to live for God's interests and the consolation of your poor and unworthy subject, who is also your most respectful and faithful servant; one who is at your feet in spirit and would wish to be so in fact, to speak with you a bit about the reign of our little King Jesus and how He came into this world, to rule in the hearts of His elect, and especially in yours, Madam. However I must bear my captivity and be content to be with you in spirit.

n. 2631

The newborn Jesus

I pray Our Lord Jesus Christ to fill you with the grace and holiness of His divine Infancy, and that your poor heart may be expanded with the love of this ineffable mystery, which impresses us with the tenderness of God's heart and the excess of His divine charity. I try to adore Him for you, Madam, but it is in such an unworthy manner that I do not dare to appear in the presence of that humbled august and supreme Majesty, although His condition as an infant veils His infinite greatness and gives us the freedom to approach Him. What gives me great confidence is that He has come to show mercy to sinners, and that He is already the victim of God's justice and holiness, to make reparation to them. In the manger He is immolated, just as on the altar and the cross. His tears and little cries appease His Father's anger, and without speaking or acting, He is meriting Paradise for us. We have only to contemplate Him in His mysterious sacrifice and unite ourselves to His Heart, His intentions, and the designs of His love for us; slipping gently and sweetly into the grace of His holy childhood, which contains infinite marvels that will cause the angels' eternal admiration and man's astonishment. O Child-God, how adorable and incomprehensible You are to the human mind! We must adore You in silence, and lose ourselves in the depths of Your holy humility, being reduced to nothing as much as possible in Your divine presence.

Madam, this is what you are doing, and all the more effectively since this excellent disposition is accompanied by suffering. That is what causes you enter into conformity of state with this Child God, who is in no way exempt from suffering in His manger. Yet I am asking Him to reduce yours, and to crown your patience, increasing your love for His goodness, with a complete trust that He will do everything good for His glory and your sanctification. Remain in peace with this firm conviction that God's Spirit is impressing on your heart. Courage! Let us go to God through the paths that He pleases, and provided that we arrive at our blessed end, that is enough; all else will sooner or later be reduced to nothing.

I pray Our Lord to strengthen you, and give you the grace to neglect nothing that you must do for Him. God alone and nothing else. If He grants my prayer, He will support you and make you dwell in Himself by a special grace. All that I am asking of you is that you remain in your precious and lovable abandonment, allowing God to act in you; and especially remain firm in the confidence that everything will work out for your good and salvation, bearing the mark of His elect, since you are crucified with Him.

n. 1314

For the feast of Christmas
Although the activity of this holy day is great, I could not fail to write to learn of your health, Fr. N. having told me that you were ill. I am anxious about it and doubly concerned because of tonight's devotions, at which you cannot assist, which will grieve you all the more, since you are accustomed to receive Communion on this feast, through which your soul shares in the grace and holiness of the ineffable mystery of the birth of God's Son in our flesh.

This is a feast which you love dearly and which resembles your heart's dispositions; it desires only pure love. There is something which enchants us in this adorable birth and which transports us with a holy ardor. We see our God reducing Himself to nothing under the figure of a baby who has nothing for His birthright except poverty, suffering, and weakness; and His love for us has reduced

Him to this. If you please, do as did St. Teresa [of Avila], see only Jesus and yourself in that excess of love, certain through faith that the mystery is uniquely for you, although it is applied to others as well. If you consider yourself as the object of God's love and mercy, which made Him descend from heaven to earth to give Himself completely to you and draw you to Himself completely, you will feel your heart so quickened with a humble gratitude and a sincere desire to give yourself absolutely to Him that, almost without your being aware of it, it will cause a heavenly blaze which will draw you out of yourself and you will burn without being aware of it. Oh, Madam, how happy your soul will be if it is burning with this sacred fire!

Beware of letting it go out. Preserve it by a deep and holy humility, being sure that the more you humble yourself, the nearer God will come to you. It is unbelievable how much God communicates Himself to souls who have been brought to nothing. Alas! If we had the courage to surrender ourselves to God as His domain, He would do great things in us, but we do not remain in holy abandonment, in faith. We want to do everything, know everything, and feel everything; whereas the soul become nothing abides in God, becoming one spirit with Him.[6] Madam, try to receive Communion to receive this grace. Give yourself to the newborn Jesus. You are His domain. He is your King and Sovereign, do not refuse Him your homage or submission. Promise Him a new faithfulness in dependence on His guidance and never cease doing what you believe He desires of you. Obey His light in the one who holds His place for you.

How many things I have to say to you, but now it is Vespers and I am leaving you to find you again immediately, in the stable, adoring the Infant God. I will stay at the holy Virgin's feet to learn from her how I must act before so astonishing a miracle, before God become a babe on a little straw between two beasts. Remain kneeling there, adoring everything He says to His Father for you, and endeavor to become His victim as He became yours in the manger. Adhere to all His designs. I must end; here is the last peal of the bell.

n. 2629

6. 1 Cor 6:17.

For the feast of the Sacred Heart of the Blessed Virgin Mary
(February 8)

I could not rest tonight without wishing you a good evening, hoping that tomorrow we will have the honor of seeing you, if the time is right, to celebrate the precious feast of the most sacred Heart of the august Mother of God.

This is a feast full of love, since that most lovable Heart was the furnace of love into which the eternal Father cast His Word to be clothed in our nature, and through His incarnation in that holy Heart, to become our victim and love us with an infinite love. O wondrous Heart! O Heart burning with pure love, let me share in your divine flames! Consume us as a holocaust with you in an odor of sweetness. Blessed is the soul who may enter into that virginal heart, and more blessed still if it receives from that Mother of grace some share in her holy dispositions. My understanding shows me the most delightful Heart of the most august Mother of God as a sacred storeroom wherein are contained all God's gifts. In it are contained all virtues in the highest perfection. If we look there for sweetness, she is entirely filled with it; for humility, she is completely reduced to nothing; for submission to the divine will, she utters a mysterious *fiat* which makes her a slave of the divine will; for patience, we have adequate proofs of this in her holy actions. But I linger the longest over her charity and kindness for sinners, whose refuge she is, and her most holy Heart is always filled with mercy to receive them and reconcile them to Jesus Christ. Our whole fortune is in her blessed hands. We are certain of blessed success when she takes a hand in our affairs. I ask her to take care of yours and that through her aid you may have all the blessings I desire for you.

Ask this holy Heart for everything you need. We will not forget N. and we will pray that her Heart may be your strength, your light, and your protection, and that you will find there all that is lacking in your affairs, and for your sanctification. I am yours, more than my own, in her. With deep respect…

n. 1202

Lent

For the season of Lent

Providence willed yesterday to take from me the honor of writing you to give you a thousand humble thanks for the trouble you took in giving me precise news about your illness: it is the only consolation that I receive in the long absence from your presence. I must suffer this sorrow in this holy season in a spirit of penance and sacrifice, by mortifying my desire; yours should not be so great, considering what I am in every way. Still I want to do as you do, submitting absolutely to God, taking all my delight in His good pleasure. However, you have the advantage in everything, and especially in resembling Our Lord Jesus Christ through suffering, since you are on the cross with Him. Also in His holy solitude, where He had no place to rest His divine head. Indeed, you are honoring that lovable Savior in His sorrowful states, and perhaps those of the spirit as much as of the body. Courage, courage! Be the victim of His pure love, and live for Him alone. It is your intention and my desire to see you completely His and this is why you must dwell in Him: "he who is not with me is against me."[1] These are His divine words. Therefore let us be completely in Him. Let us move and act only by His spirit and for His pleasure and we will have a wondrous peace, known only by those who possess it.

O infinite happiness, how rare you are! Why is this? It is because the creature does not know how to entrust herself completely in holy abandonment to God, because she does not have enough confidence in His kindness, or patience to wait for it. Blessed abandonment, wherein the soul is divinely sustained! God is her life, her strength, and her support without her knowing it. If the beginning of this state is dark, what follows becomes wholly luminous. God

---

1. Mt 12:30.

gives Himself to the soul and drawing this soul entirely to Himself, it becomes one single thing with Him: I am right to say therefore that such a soul has an infinite happiness.

This is enough, I do not know what I am saying; it is to amuse you a little, since you will experience it much more than I. I am eager to know how you fared tonight.

n. 1910

Immolation in Jesus suffering

I cannot go through the day without telling you that I am very sorrowful about your continued illness; and I am the more affected because I want to relieve you of it without diminishing your merit and the benefits your soul receives from it at all. It was necessary that it increase again so that your cross might be fulfilled, that is, that both the interior and the exterior should suffer at present, in order to be immolated with Jesus, on Calvary and on the altar, through a conformity of state. I see that it is all His delight to apply you to His sorrowful love and cause you to bear the signs of it. Dare I say, Madam, that I suffer them with you and share in your afflictions of body and soul, regarding you as a victim at the stake. Cast your loving gaze on the divine sun who must enkindle its fire and consume your being. Madam, I see you in your usual sweetness, edifying all those around you who have no other consolation than offering you their compassion. Oh, what sorrow to see the one we love suffering! It would be a thousand times easier to suffer oneself. Alas! I would regard myself blessed to take your sufferings myself! If I knew how to worthily and piously bear crosses like you, I would hope that God would give me the grace to share in yours, but I am too great a sinner; that is why He does not grant my prayers. I beg Him at least to increase His graces with such abundance that your heart is entirely inebriated with His love and your senses are so enraptured with His delights and ineffable communications that you are absorbed in them. This is the wish of one who is poor and powerless, and who is all yours in Jesus. With profound respect...

n. 1122

On Jesus's suffering

Madam, I understand that your sickness and the bad weather deprive me of the honor of seeing you, but it is much better for me to be mortified than to increase your pains for one moment. Madam, this is how Our Lord is making you enter into this holy season of penance, in union with His states. Ask Him to sanctify it in you. Here we have adopted three states or dispositions of our divine Savior to honor and imitate Him during these forty days. I think that you would be glad to share in them and put them into practice.

The first is the solitude of Jesus in the desert and in the Holy Sacrament of the altar; the second is His penitence; the third is His sorrowful death.

We must honor these three states in Jesus which are contained in His penitence. Yet since you are entirely full of these good thoughts and always occupied in a holy way, one little word is enough to give you material for an inner conversation on the subject. If I have the privilege of seeing you tomorrow, we will discuss the rest.

I ask Our Lord to give you better health and all the blessings I wish for you.

n. 854

Conformity to Jesus suffering

Your illness gives me much anxiety; however my grief cannot exempt you from it. God, who wants to sanctify you, is making you share in the cross, now in one way, now in another. He plays with the elect, and one writer said that "sufferings are the games of divine love," and that "God delights in a soul who suffers and never turns away His gaze from that lovable object." See the benefit the cross gives you. It purifies you; it makes you worthy of God's approach, and opens paradise for you. Blessed sufferings which produce such wondrous effects! Our Lord gives you a share of His and although I know little of their excellence, I would like the power to draw them into my heart to relieve yours—nonetheless without depriving you of the merit.

I see I must be resolved to do without the honor of seeing you and that it is not proper for me to aspire to such a valuable favor. I must remain in my nothingness and be content with declaring to you with a thousand profound respects that I am unworthy of all your kindness.

n. 2982

Conformity and abandonment to God in crosses

I am delighted to see that you always take the good part: to serve God and to love Him is to reign. It is true that you are sacrificing a great deal, but also that you will find an ample recompense. If your birth is not accompanied by all the advantages it deserves on earth, Heaven will grant a hundredfold. Do not be grieved, but join yourself more and more to Jesus Christ. With all your heart, enter into His designs for yourself and your house. I cannot believe that He would allow it to perish. He will restore its glory. We must wait on His timing; everything is in God. You see it—the cares and industry of creatures do not advance it at all.

We should always have recourse to the august Mother of God; she is the queen of your Dominions, and she will not allow them to be destroyed. Hand them over entirely to her care, and you, take refuge in her most holy and sacred Heart with your dear children. That is a refuge which will always be most favorable to you and you will obtain from it all that you ask in Jesus Christ. That precious solitude will be for you a place of repose and delight. There divine love will be your strength, and nothing will be able to shake your courage while you are under the wings of that gracious Mother. Still allow me to beg you that we renew our devotion to her, so that you may declare your confidence in her once more. God gives to us according to our faith and, since He has granted you the grace to prefer His most Holy Will in everything, it will take care of all that affects you. Nonetheless, do what you can to not be cast down about events contrary to your desires. Be resolute on your cross to which God's good pleasure fixes you; there His love should be your consummation just as His grace will be your support. In this continual sacrifice you will be sanctified and you will become one and the same victim with Jesus Christ. I am not ceasing to pray with all my heart for its pain and bitterness to be sweetened, since I feel everything that affects you in the depth of my heart.

n. 1490

On the sufferings of Jesus

Madam, I do not doubt at all that you have a new fervor of love in these Holy Days, and that the sight of the suffering Jesus is the precious object occupying all your thoughts. I beg Him to fill you with graces and blessings in your precious solitude.

On our part, we will offer to Him the privation of your dear presence, which we are enduring as a very severe penance. I hope that Our Lord will agree to this, Madam, since it is harsh to be so long separated for a heart which has received from yours so many signs and proofs of your kindness. I will not forget you and will try to see you in spirit in the Cenacle and on Calvary, where I believe you will be more than anywhere else.

I embrace your feet with profound respect, awaiting a holy Resurrection which will make me more worthy to enjoy your presence. See how I cannot prevent myself from telling you of my displeasure. From this you will conclude that I am not dead and see my imperfection and that I am so strongly attached to you, Madam, that I can only be separated from you with great sorrow.

n. 1077

Let us suffer with Jesus

Madam, I would be very consoled if I had the honor of seeing you, being anxious about your illness. With all my heart I wish to have all your pains, so as to relieve you a little in the crosses that are renewed every day. Certainly, we must conclude that God desires great sanctity for you, since He keeps you in such crucifying conditions, such that it may be said they are without pause and without end. Your consolation must be entirely in Our Lord who suffered from the first moment of His Incarnation; and you, Madam, through likeness of state to Him, are in the number of those who have carried the Lord's yoke from their youth. Take heart, then, heaven will end all the evils of this life and you will have no greater joy than to have suffered in this world out of love and conformity to Jesus Christ Our Lord.

n. 1424

Easter

On the feast of Easter (1)

I could not reply to you yesterday evening about what you did me the honor of writing to me, and I cannot read it without having a renewed wonder at it, being unable to comprehend your kindness. Alas! If you sometimes receive good effects from our conversations, that is the reward for your humility which lowers itself to the point of allowing (at its feet) [at your feet], a sinner which the earth should swallow up. It is not the things I tell you that are strengthening you but the grace of the one who is hidden in you, like the leaven in the parable of the gospel, hidden in the three measures of flour. It is Jesus, your heart's only love, who supports you and animates you with His spirit, and is drawing you completely to Himself, by His divine operation, in the secret of your soul. It is He who keeps you in a place of refuge and solitude, while waiting until He can separate you entirely from creatures. He knows that such are the most tender sentiments of your heart, and that it has already taken its flight into the clefts of the rock,[1] which are the wounds of Jesus's sacred Humanity; and that in those precious caverns you mourn ceaselessly for the enjoyment of the one who has wounded your heart with the arrows of His divine love, and that it cannot rejoice in anything on earth but that delightful union.

"Taste and see how the Lord is sweet and gentle."[2] I pray that He will make you experience the effect of His divine words which the Gospel gives us today as the subject of our mediation. That lovable Savior says to us, "When I am lifted up from the earth, I will draw everything to Myself."[3] O blessed drawing which tears us away from

1. Cf. Song of Songs 2:14.
2. Ps 33:9.
3. Jn 12:32.

32

the earth of ourselves, to unite us and transform us entirely in Jesus! Madam, let us beseech Him to exalt Himself in us, so that He might draw us entirely to Himself. I asked Him for that favor for you this morning at Communion. I believe He will grant it generously and lovingly, since it is consonant with your desires and the fervor that inwardly consumes you.

I am restraining my pen, which would annoy on account of the abundance of my feeling for you. I should leave you to adore that sacred Calvary whereon is the cross of my divine Master and Savior, since tomorrow I will have the honor of seeing you adore Him on His Eucharistic throne, where love will immolate Him for you and will draw you into His sacrifice, to be made a single victim with Him. It is in that mystery of glory and humiliation that I am yours with a most sincere heart.

With profound respect...

n. 1145

On the feast of Easter (2)

I thank you a thousand times for the honor you did me yesterday. Today I wish you a glorious Resurrection and desire it for you as a member of Jesus Christ, which shares in the benefits of that divine head, and is no longer animated except with His life. *Non quae super terram.*[4] He is no longer on earth, that is why we must not stop there.

Let us go to seek Him in Himself, in the most holy Sacrament of the altar, where every day He renews His holy and adorable mysteries. With all my heart I beg Him to produce their effects in your soul, even as I would like to have them in myself. May that adorable Savior cause you to enter into His new life which separates you from the old man, so as to live in Him. My God, when will Jesus reign in us so completely that He will find His repose in us and be triumphant over our whole being? There is neither good, nor joy, nor consolation apart from this disposition: to be subject to Jesus is to reign gloriously. We are His conquests; He has ransomed us at an infinite price, it is a matter of justice for Him to possess us absolutely. Henceforth

4. Col 3:2. Mind the things that are above, not the things that are upon the earth.

we must not refuse Him anything, everything is His. Yet we can also say that He is all ours and that in Him we lack nothing. May Jesus live and reign glorious and triumphant in our hearts! Amen.

n. 407

On the Resurrection (1)

I received with great joy the honor you did me, giving me news of your health, and was very sad because of your fatigue from these Holy Days. I thank you for your continued kindness for our affairs in Rome.[5] If it is successful, it is to you that I owe all my gratitude, after God. I am certain that the most Holy Sacrament will repay your zeal. It is for His glory that you are working ceaselessly. If my poor prayer is heard, you will be filled with heavenly blessings, knowing that earthly ones have no charm for your heart, which has no desire to live any life but that of Jesus resurrected and has no taste except for the things of heaven.

I ask that adorable Savior to draw you so powerfully that you will enter into Him, to live from His love in Him, and bring to perfection in you the grace and holiness of His adorable mysteries.

I am yours in the respect which humbles me at your feet...

n. 741

On the Resurrection (2)

I am eager to hear the news about your health, Madam, and if your cold persists.[6] I would be especially grieved about it if it deprived us of the consolation of embracing your feet and of the honor of seeing you dine in the little house of the Holy Sacrament whose little servants would rejoice greatly in your most honored presence, who long for this happiness, and myself more than the others. I desire to know if you have entered into this mystery which we adore, and

5. This is perhaps an allusion to the solicitations made by the Duchess of Orléans through the intervention of her ambassador in the Court at Rome, to obtain the approval of the Constitutions. (Cf. Catherine de Bar, *Documents Historiques*, p. 237 and following.)

6. MS N267 stops here and picks up again at "to know if you entered..."; completed via MS P110.

which is filled with so many graces that I cannot help but wish their fullness for you. My zeal for your soul and sanctification is always great. And I can say that I wish to give my own life to establish you in the highest sanctity that God is asking of you, which is nothing other than the result of the mystery of the Resurrection, which causes us to live Jesus Christ's new life.

Oh! How divine that life is! Please God that we were all animated with it; our heart and our mind would behave in a very different manner. Jesus would be the source and we would not see or desire anything apart from Him. However, in order to receive this favor we must be faithful to the Holy Spirit's working. We must remain hidden in Jesus Christ as He says Himself in these holy words, "The one who remains in Me and I in Him will bear much fruit."[7] These are the words of life. Therefore, let us remain in Jesus and let us be so hidden in Him that we cannot be found, so that we can say in truth, "*non quae super terram*."[8] Certainly one must think seriously about belonging wholly to God through Jesus Christ.

n. 1464

On the Gospel of the Good Shepherd

I ask for news of your health and if the gospel of the day has not expanded your heart, seeing itself under the guidance of so good a Shepherd, who gives His life for His sheep, among which you are numbered.

I beseech you, grant love the freedom to bring about transports of joy and gratitude: for the care and tenderness, and for the infinite mercies of this good Shepherd who has protected you from falling prey to the devil for so many years. Turn your eyes to the adorable Heart of this divine Shepherd; you will see that it is completely overflowing with love for you, completely focused on you, and completely sacrificed to His Father for you. Listen to His holy voice in the depths of your heart: He tells you interiorly that He is the way, the truth, and the life. We need nothing but this. Let us follow that lovable Shepherd. His sheep hear His voice and follow Him. If

7. Jn 14:5.
8. Col 3:2.

we listen to Him we will hear Him and if we are faithful we will follow Him. Oh, the happiness of following Jesus! He is the way, and the path in which we must walk, the truth which we must believe, and the life which must animate us. I would to God that these three truths be impressed on our hearts and that we may bring forth their fruits! Oh, how blessed we would be to walk in Jesus, to believe in Jesus in all His sacred mysteries and His divine words, and to live from Jesus. Experience this happiness; you can and should do so as a faithful sheep of our good Shepherd's flock.

A soul who lives by the spirit of our holy gospel has nothing but joy and repose in God. Feed on Jesus Christ and for His love, do not refuse me the quarter of an hour [of prayer] that I ask of you. Present yourself before His holy presence every day, to receive in your soul the impressions of His grace and enter into a disposition of faith, love, and reverence regarding this infallible and powerful truth, which contains everything: God is, and this is enough for a Christian soul. If you wish to carry out this little exercise every day, I will take the liberty of writing to you about how you should proceed. I am certain that your soul will receive great blessings from it, and that if you continue, you will be able to pray for many hours without difficulty. Grant me this favor and let your humility permit me to ask for an account of it sometimes, to see if Our Lord is making an impression on your soul. If you enter into this in the way that is necessary, you will make light of the world and all it contains.

Forgive my zeal; I will gladly tell you that you are more in my heart than I am myself, but this is to give you continually to Jesus and His holy Mother.

n. 964

Ascension

On the Ascension

Allow me to say you should prepare to depart tomorrow with our lovable Savior who is returning to His Father. There is no possibility of allowing Him to go alone. We must do our utmost to accompany Him in spirit, and hide our hearts in His, to live no longer except with His life.

Today you can say in truth that your "kingdom is not of this world,"[1] that you willingly leave it in order to follow Jesus Christ and return with Him to your heavenly fatherland. You have come from God and you must return to Him. This is your motto; remember it always and take care that nothing prevents you from entering into this glorious center.

As the body follows the head, so we must follow Our Lord into heaven. Alas! Who could remain on the earth without Him? That is the lament of the saints in this life and it is a real hell to them to be separated from that divine object for one moment. With the righteous, let us long and desire to be, as St. Paul said, "freed from the bonds of our captivity." Oh! How good it would be to die tomorrow! Heaven is opened and Jesus makes His triumphal entry into it—we could easily enter with Him. The mercies are abundant and the eternal Father, so occupied in delighting in His Son's glory, will not reject those who will be entering with Him.

I do not know if you will come tomorrow to adore our good Master and receive His blessing at the hour that He rises to heaven; I hope for it from your piety, if your health allows it. I desire it with the same heart with which I am [yours] with profound respect…

n. 7

1. Cf. Jn 18:36.

37

For the Ascension

If I did not mortify my inclination, you would often be bothered by your little servant, for the sake of having news about your health and if the quarter of an hour is not forgotten. You promised to be faithful to it. From time to time I will remind you about it. You must not be discouraged about it if it does not come easily at the beginning; what follows will soften the pain.

I beseech you to make use of these three days to prepare for following our adorable Savior into heaven. We must not remain on earth. The body must always accompany the head. I beg you to do a little reading on the mystery of the Ascension in Fr. Bourgoing[2] or Hayneuve,[3] so that your soul is filled with it and your love renewed. Oh! When will we be separated from the world and creatures? When will we go into our heavenly fatherland? We are poor exiles on earth and in a foreign country. Yet we rejoice in the hope that all our trials will someday end and that we will go to our Father's house to love and possess Him eternally. Oh, what joy to see God and to be transformed in Him forever!

Therefore, let us be faithful and courageous. Let us live only for Jesus. It is in Him that I am yours...

n. 2685

2. Francois Bourgoing (1585–1662), born in Paris into a famous law family. One of the first companions of Cardinal de Bérulle, he succeeded him as the third general of the Oratory (1641–1662). He founded ten houses in France and Flanders. He wrote many works, one of which Mother Mectilde cites here: *Truths and Excellences of Jesus Christ Our Lord Arranged in Meditations for All the Days of the Year* (see *DTC* fasc. XIII col. 1099).

3. Julien Hayneuve (1588–1663), born at Laval; entered the novitiate of the Company of Jesus on May 31, 1608. An ascetic theologian, he was one of the masters of the spiritual life in the seventeenth century. The work cited here is *Meditations on the Life of Jesus Christ for Every Day of the Year and the Feasts of the Saints*, four volumes in quarto, Paris, 1611–1642 (see *DTC* fasc. XLVIII col. 2069).

Pentecost

For the feast of Pentecost (1)

I do not dare to hope for the honor of seeing you today; that is why I am sending you the letter that I just received, asking for news of your health and if the quarter of an hour continues. You must not stop for anything. It is for God and to God directly that you are giving it, and this is why you must be faithful to it. If you please, make use of it during this octave to offer yourself to the power and love of the Holy Spirit, simplifying your thoughts to remain in a simple attention and abandonment to His grace and operations, adoring Him in silence. Meekly receive what it will please Him to do and be docile to His inspirations. He will not fail to give you some, and illuminate your mind about the gospel truths, and inflame your will to practice them generously.

My God, how hard it is to endure this life when we see the dangers with which we are surrounded and how easy it is to be separated from God! I have a great longing to die, in order to no longer offend Him and have the blessing of being nourished in eternity with those beauties and splendors of Jesus Christ's mysteries. Oh! How good it is to be to occupied with them and how much better to bear their fruits in our souls! Nothing can satisfy us in this life, because it contains nothing worthy of a soul created to be eternally occupied with Jesus, and consumed in His love. Madam, let us make the resolution, while awaiting deliverance from our captivity, not to live except in the love, from the love, and for the love of Jesus. Since we have received the God of love, who is the Holy Spirit, let us not live except through love, which unites us and transforms us completely in Jesus, for time and eternity.

n. 1274

For the feast of Pentecost (2)

If I had received the Holy Spirit, I would have the gift of giving you joy by enkindling in you His utterly divine fire. Only a spark would be needed to consume everything which causes Him sorrow and to carry us away into God's Heart; to have but one breath and one will with that adorable Heart. Madam, there you must find the strength and courage you need to endure the many blows that divine Providence is constantly releasing on you. If He wounds you, He can heal you; and if He kills you, He will bring you back to life. Let us have some faith and trust. If He were to swallow up and consume all that we are, we should act like St. Augustine, because our faith would become stronger. And if everything were lost without hope, then we must believe more constantly, because faith is not pure when there is some evidence; but it is pure and naked when everything human is destroyed; and it is by means of and on account of such faith in God that Our Lord does miracles. We must hope for them from His kindness, at the time when it pleases Him to perform them for His glory.

Be strong and constant, Madam, in a simple, loving regard toward God. Wait for those moments. If you can moderate your natural activity a bit, you will have a little repose. I wish you the fullness of peace and grace, with a perfect submission to the reign of Jesus Christ.

n. 2683

Holy Trinity

For the feast of the Holy Trinity (1)

I am taking the liberty of telling you that tomorrow is the feast of your soul, in which the three divine Persons dwell as in a temple. At Holy Communion, remember to renew your holy vows of baptism and give thanks to God for the vocation to the faith. I entreat you to celebrate this august feast worthily, renewing the dedication which Jesus has made [of you] to the Holy Trinity. You will observe, therefore, that you are not your own, or at your own disposal; that you are God's through Jesus, and that you do not possess one breath that is not consecrated to Him. Live in this spirit of faith and tend more than ever to be detached from yourself. Hand over everything to God. Think of loving Him and He will attend to all your needs, because His desire is that you be His without reservation, that you rest in His love.

I beg your pardon for my very great liberty, but your kindness is the cause of it. I am, with the deepest respect, all yours.

n. 1296

For the feast of the Holy Trinity (2)

Praised be God for the news that your health is better! You must remain well until Thursday to celebrate the feast of the completion[1] of Jesus's love toward men. Oh! How great and profound is this mystery for Christian souls! The feast we celebrate tomorrow is beyond words: we must adore it without comprehending it, submitting with a deep humility to the proposed truth of the august and undivided Trinity. But since this feast is better celebrated in heaven than on earth, we will apply our heart and mind to celebrating it

---

1. *Epuisement*—exhaustion; the feast of His loving "to the end."

magnificently in our soul. It is the feast of the Dedication of the mystical temple.

We know by faith that the Christian's heart is the temple of the living God: the Apostle assures us of it.[2] The Church teaches us that this inner temple is dedicated and consecrated in baptism to the Holy Trinity through Jesus Christ, and that the three divine Persons, the Father, the Son, and the Holy Spirit, dwell continually in this temple, and never leave it, whatever may happen during the course of this life. This being a dogma of faith, we need only recollect ourselves, therefore, in order to adore the august Trinity in our souls, presenting our worship and sacrifices to Him. Among these, the most excellent is to be immolated for His glory unceasingly, through Jesus Christ, who will present us to His Father.

The first consideration is to see our soul's dignity and how it belongs irrevocably to the Most Holy Trinity.

The second is that, since the Holy Trinity is always in us, we must always be in Him, and accomplish in our souls Jesus's words to the Samaritan woman when He said, "The time is coming that the Father would have adorers who adore Him in spirit and in truth,"[3] not only in Jerusalem, but everywhere and above all in ourselves: in spirit by faith, and in truth, from the depths of the heart through love, and deeply and sincerely reducing ourselves to nothing before that Supreme Majesty.

The third will be to inquire of our soul what are its duties before that ineffable deity—to inquire if it believes Him to be in it; if it adores Him, and if it refers itself and all its operations to Him; if it sees itself and considers itself as constantly dependent on divine help, the inexhaustible wellspring of grace and holiness hidden in it. In consequence of these little considerations and reflections, you will know if you are giving to God the worship and reverence you owe Him in His interior temple. And if you see that you have failed in this, make a fitting atonement for it to the Most Holy Trinity, and renew the vows and promises made in baptism to oblige yourself to a more perfect fidelity.

2. 1 Cor 3:16.
3. Jn 4:23.

Holy Trinity

You see that I am trying to do what I promised you, to rouse you from time to time and encourage new fervor. I suppose you know about this a thousand times more than I do since I am only a poor wretch who deserves to be eternally humbled. In speaking, I am obeying your command to me and giving you an opportunity to exercise your humility and patience, and to become a great saint. And this is what I wish and desire for you with fervor and respect.

n. 64

Corpus Christi

For the feast of Corpus Christi (1)

I do not need to arouse your heart to the love of our adorable and most noble Mystery; I know perfectly well that it is your life and your soul's happiness; and that your soul has no greater joy than to be consumed in His holy Presence, in love and adoration, doing here below what the angels and the blessed do in heaven. Oh, what a gift the eternal Father has given us! Oh, what kindness in Jesus to will to remain with us until the end of the ages! A God with us, never withdrawing, although the ingratitude of men would oblige Him to abandon them. O great and excessive charity! He must truly be carried away with love to remain among sinners who only have the wickedness to offend His goodness! One is overcome at the sight of that abyss of mercy and rendered dumb. Oh! How can we not die of love at the love of this infinitely lovable God of love!

This great and wondrous feast can only be worthily celebrated by love, which I separate into two actions:

Love is grateful for the infinite graces God has placed in the divine Eucharist for us and especially for the ineffable gift He makes to us of all Himself.

And love transforms the soul and unites it to Jesus Christ, who pours Himself out completely in love in this glorious Sacrament, which is the goal of its institution.

In it, He gives us everything without any reserve. God has nothing in Himself that He does not give us in Holy Communion; likewise, we should have nothing in ourselves, or outside of ourselves, which we do not give Him upon receiving Him. He enters into us so that we might enter into Him. He spends His sacramental being in us, that our life be consumed in Him. He lowers Himself to elevate us. He sacrifices Himself in us, so as to sacrifice us in Himself. He wants to live in us so that we may live in Him and through Him.

44

You are completely filled with the lights of this great mystery; it remains only for me to ask Our Lord Jesus Christ to make you bear its fruits. It belongs to Him to produce them and this is what He desires if we do not prevent it.

I take the humble boldness of commending myself to your holy prayers. It seems to me that I feel a little interior ambition to begin to do better; but I know that if the spirit is willing, the flesh is weak, therefore I need to be supported. I hope that this holy octave will not pass without our having the honor of embracing your feet many times. In the meanwhile, I wish you every blessing from the adorable Eucharist.

n. 1027

For the feast of Corpus Christi (2)

Is it possible that, in the midst of your sufferings, your kindness can think of your most unworthy servant? I am amazed. This is the effect of a very great charity. Would to God I could take into my heart all the pains that you suffer; I would have a singular satisfaction.

My God, what a delight it is to love the Son of God in the Most Holy Sacrament! My soul is carried away with wonder at His unspeakable mercies; he allows us not only to say that we love Him, but desires to be our food. He descends to us in order to raise us to Himself, and fill us with the most wonderful favors. I cannot help but cry out: O my adorable Savior, how good You are, with infinite goodness! Madam, you know this and you experience it more purely than I. I know the delights and charms of your heart, which has no greater joy in this world than to render to Him its adoration, before His altars. It is a great joy when I have the honor to see you doing so in this house. I think Our Lord receives with pleasure the homage that you render Him and which I offer to Him frequently in reparation for my negligence and lack of devotion. Continue this homage, Madam; you will receive great blessings from it.

In heaven the person will never be without glory who honored and confessed Jesus Christ on earth under the sacramental species. I regard you as a predestined soul and the beloved of Our Lord in the Most Holy Sacrament. Love Him as much as you can in this Mys-

45

tery since it is the one in which He endures the most humiliation. Hide yourself in that sacred ciborium with Him, and be buried under the accidents [of bread and wine] as a result of love which keeps you united to Him there, living with the hidden life of Jesus, for His Father's glory. Live for Him alone; this is His intention in the holy Eucharist, and it is for this reason that He comes to us. I ask Him to draw you more and more into His holy love and that no creature be any more in you. Let Jesus alone live in you and possess the whole. This is the wish of the one who knows that you value nothing in this world except Jesus Christ, in whom I am yours with deep respect...

n. 410

For the feast of Corpus Christi (3)

I am very troubled about your health. If you had been able to come to adore the most Holy Sacrament which was exposed in our church, you would have received a heavenly strength to bear life's sorrows and continual griefs. I desire the consolation of seeing you here more than usual, since it seems to me that your soul would receive many graces and mercies here.

In the condition in which divine Providence keeps you at present, wherein you have need of God's support—creatures not having the power to provide this—God alone can rejoice and console your heart, and you experience this. You will find it fully in the adorable Sacrament of the altar, where love confines Him, to give us the means of approaching Him, and to find a paradise on earth, while awaiting our entrance into heaven, possessing Him with the blessed, through the beatific vision. You must finish your penance in the captivity where you are, hoping that He will open to you the door of sacred repose, for which your soul longs so fervently.

I am praying to Our Lord Jesus Christ that this may be soon, so that you can taste, before death, the joys of a heart which enjoys God, which possesses Him and is possessed by Him, and which, through that divine union, sees itself entirely separated from all creatures. I think that this is the state to which your desires tend and in which you wish to be firmly established. It is a great grace to comprehend its greatness, excellence, and merit. It is still greater to

46

long for it with all our strength insofar as God desires it. At least tend toward it through love and desire, by a holy detachment from what is not God, gently separating yourself from what is burdening your mind, so as to preserve peace and tranquility of heart, which is so necessary for the sweet enjoyment of God's presence.

The memory of the precious person whom God has placed in His paradise and your present feelings will not prevent you from becoming a great saint. You are offering sacrifices to God for this, which will be very pleasing to Him. This is what you are doing with a holy humility. It must be accompanied with perseverance.

I beg a thousand pardons for the liberty I am taking in writing to you in this manner. I am, with very deep respect…

n. 1514

The Sacred Heart of Jesus

The Heart of Jesus is our repose

You did me a great favor yesterday by reassuring me about your health. This is a piece of news which gives me great joy. I pray Our Lord that He will maintain it. Yet with all the blessings that I wish for you, you will be in a perfect repose through a holy union and transformation in the Sacred Heart of Jesus, which is the blessed center of your soul; to this you have been aspiring for so long. In fact that is the true and essential repose.

The whole earth and creatures are nothing but bitterness and affliction of spirit, you know this. And the deepest regret of our soul at death will be not having detached our heart from everything created and having often preferred created things to the love of Jesus, allowing our mind to be too much occupied with human things. Let us go to God every day, with a holy resolution to do nothing except for Him, to desire nothing apart from Him, and to love nothing except in Him.

Let us see and do everything in that adorable immensity in which we swim like a sponge in the sea. To whatever side we turn we are in God; we move, we live, we breathe in Him, but this is often without thinking about it. Let us beware of continuing our little negligences and hasten to become attentive to that wonderful Presence. Jesus truly deserves our regard. It is necessary to pause frequently before this divine object and remember the precious lesson that God gave Abraham: "Walk in my presence and you will be perfect." Here is a very congenial, very gentle, and very sweet law of perfection. By becoming faithful to it, we will participate in the saints' supreme happiness, which is to possess God in this world by faith, while waiting to possess Him in Heaven in glory. A soul who does not take any satisfaction in earthly things anymore does not have much trouble conversing with God and finding all its satisfaction in Him.

Rejoice to have no more joys among creatures, so that henceforth you may take them all in the one who loves you with an infinite and eternal love.

I am asking Him to consume you with His most precious flames, and to make me worthy of being, with all the profound respect I owe you, all yours.

n. 3097

On the Holy Eucharist

On our Institute

I have always believed that God wanted to make use of you to honor His Son Jesus Christ in our Institute and that He desires to crown you in heaven for the sake of the glory you procure for Him on earth; establishing the perpetual adoration we have professed which could not exist for long years except through our Congregation maintaining it.

If Our Lord accomplishes the words He gave you, we will be very happy; but it will be to your kindness and piety only that we will be indebted and to which we will owe eternal thanks. This required zeal as great as yours and an authority as powerful. I pray that God may make us worthy of giving thanks for these singular graces, but effectively, in His presence. We will not cease to ask Our Lord Jesus Christ in the divine Sacrament of the altar to give you all the blessings I have desired for you so long, and above all a completely child-like and loving trust in Jesus Christ. And this so that He may cause you to experience the tenderness of His divine Heart and that He may powerfully draw yours, through the strength of His pure love, in such a way that you find your repose in a sweet abandonment to His good pleasure, so that your soul may be like a little child of His holy Providence, without any worry and without any desires beyond a simple adherence to His love.

This is what Our Lord wishes of you and in it you will find perfect peace of heart and a holy detachment from everything that can trouble it. I do not know if I dare to ask for news of the quarter of an hour and if it is still being practiced?

If you endure my importunities, I will sometimes rouse you to amuse you a bit, at the same time waiting for Our Lord to inspire you to honor us with your presence. While awaiting this favor, I am with profound respect...   *n.* 836

The solitude of Jesus in the Blessed Sacrament

It is true, Madam, that on your account Mr. N. granted us our request. This is a favor that we owe to your kindness. Without your authority we would never have dared to hope for it. N. will come to you to present our humble thanks. We are very much obliged to redouble our prayers for your preservation and the success of your pious intentions. If we were worthy of being heard, the vapors which trouble you would be dissipated; but they are of such a kind that only the eternal sun can destroy them. I am all the more convinced of this since human remedies have not been able to heal them up to now. Hence, it is for Jesus to work His adorable effects on the soul and body, and to enkindle the heavenly fire that He said He came to bring from heaven to earth and to burn and consume the hearts of His elect.

Madam, you are blessed if you burn with those precious flames. I beseech you to make no opposition to them, and since infirmity keeps you solitary, may the love of Jesus be your occupation. To succeed in this profitably, humble yourself before that infinite Majesty, even to the abyss of nothingness. The more your soul is little in His presence, the more He will delight in you and His graces will abound the more. Madam, through your captivity honor that of Jesus in the Eucharist. In spirit, hide yourself in the sacred ciborium with Him. Try to never leave Him in this world, since you must be with Him eternally. We must learn to love Him on earth to continue to do so in heaven.

I pray Him to grant you a good night and a new life of grace and holiness. I embrace your feet with profound respect.

n. 486

One must not draw back from Holy Communion

Allow me to say that you are still too burdened and that you listen to too much evil. You have not returned enough to God. Do you not know that it is only His goodness that can protect you and that you must hope for nothing except through His most holy Mother, who can obtain everything you need? You are not drawing enough strength from the place it is to be found. Frequent Communion is absolutely necessary for you and you are not receiving it often enough. You are drowning and sinking in reflection and this is not where you will find strength and the remedy [for your woes]. It is good to have recourse to God and receive Him. You must not dispense yourself from it [Communion] if you do not want to cause an infinite loss. Where will you find light other than in that divine Sacrament? And the grace to act as He desires, in the spirit of that divine Jesus? You can only have this in frequent Communion, and your heart should only long for that Eucharistic bread. You feel your need sufficiently. I assure you that God desires this of you, and that if you are faithful to it you will receive effects of grace which are beyond words. With the same heart that I desire these for you, I am, with all respect…

n. 2464

That Jesus may live in you and you be lost in Him

Madam, I cannot go through these Holy Days without wishing you all the graces contained in our precious mysteries. The mystery which we celebrate today is the completion of Jesus's love; one cannot think of it without a heavenly astonishment. The prophet contemplating the works of God was completely beside himself, unable to comprehend the humility of God's high and supreme majesty when He became man.

I think that the divine Eucharist is a matter for a greater rapture, since in it we adore a God so smitten with love for His poor creature that He finds the means to dwell with her until the end of the ages, and to produce the fruits of His ineffable mysteries every day. We preach the marvels of this sacrament of love frequently, but all that the science of theology can say about it is below what faith understands. After God reduces Himself to nothing under the Species, in order to enter our hearts, there is no way to ever distrust His goodness. We should not have any disposition but love, it being a certitude of faith that the one who gives the most will not refuse to give the least. I say that the gifts of God and His favors, and even beatitude, which are less than God, He will not refuse us, since He gives Himself with so much love and tenderness that I do not know how the soul can contain Him without dying. Your Royal Highness is more able to receive this grace than I am to speak about it.

On the Holy Eucharist

Madam, taste the sweetness of Jesus's Heart in Holy Communion, fulfill His desires, which He expresses through these words: "Desiderio desideravi."[1] He asks only to be received; do not deprive Him of satisfaction since He delights to converse with the children of men. And since He comes into you through this heavenly eating, enter into Him through a profound surrender of your whole self. This is the effect of *Pascha*, which is the passage of Jesus, so that Jesus may live in you and that your soul may be entirely lost in Him. Madam, this is the supreme good that I wish for you, and what time permits me to write. I know that your Royal Highness has no need to be awakened, her heart has too much love for Jesus; but it is to divert you a little, and to assure you, Madam, that I am remembering to have prayers said to God for all that concerns you, and that I would forget myself sooner than your intentions.

I am told that you will honor us with your presence, to fill our feast with blessings. I humbly ask for a share in your holy prayers.

n. 1123[2]

1. Cf. Lk 22:5.
2. Presented according to MS N258, 233.

The Company of Saints

For the feast of St. Elizabeth[1]

With all my heart I asked the holy Virgin to visit you for the accomplishment of your sanctification and perfection as effectively as she did for St. Elizabeth. I do not know if you have received the blessings I wanted for you. Oh! How good it is to welcome the Mother and the Child in this way!

We are right to say with surprise, "Unde hoc mihi?"[2] After such a visit, we should not worry about anything, inasmuch as we have in Jesus and Mary everything we can desire. A heart would be very greedy for which Jesus and His blessed Mother were not enough. Happy the soul who is never separated from them, who preserves their presence, and who can keep them in herself, so as to remember them at every moment and be set alight by their sweet conversation, with the most ardent flames of holy love! This is the intention and goal of their very precious visit. We see how St. John was set ablaze in the womb of his mother. It is through this heavenly fire that St. Elizabeth prophesied, and through this same visit in Holy Communion we should be changed and transformed into Jesus.

Madam, let us learn, let us learn well, the exercise of this glorious love which has so much power that the one who loves is permitted to do what he wills. This is what St. Augustine assures us. If my desires were heard, we would certainly be burning with that love, and we would say with St. Paul, "We no longer live, rather it is Jesus who lives in us."[3] Oh, what happiness if this were so! We would be above Fortune and the age, above creation and everything which

---

1. Another manuscript reads "for the feast of the Visitation of the Virgin."
2. Lk 1:43, Elizabeth's word to Mary: "Why is it granted to me, that the mother of my Lord should come to me?"
3. Cf. Gal 2:20.

might happen. We would be in God, with Jesus and in Jesus. We would live with His life, and we would be animated with His spirit. What would we have to fear or desire any longer in this world? Everything would be indifferent to us; we would leave the dead to bury the dead, and God would be for us all in all.[4]

There is a great delight in thinking about the benefits for a soul who lives this way, or to put it better, who has passed into Jesus Christ. Meanwhile, this is what you and I should long for humbly and fervently. Your whole inclination should be toward entering into your center which is God, and to suffer and act only for this purpose, making light of all the rest. Keep your spirit free and detached, in such a way that nothing prevents its flight toward the unique object of its love.

That is enough of this little lesson until our precious meeting, which will happen when it pleases divine Providence and your health permits.

Declaring to you that I will always be with profound respect...

n. 738

For the feast of St. Denis

Yes, Madam, the Blessed Sacrament is to be exposed tomorrow in our church thanks to the financial support of N., who became a daughter of the Church on that day.

I give thanks to Our Lord for your health and I am begging Him insistently to improve it to the point I desire, so that you can use it for the glory of God and your sanctification. I believe that you think of this every day, and do not pass any moment of life without aspiring to the holiness to which Jesus Christ's grace calls you and destined you. I pray the great St. Denis to give you a little share of his spirit of prayer, and in the perfect love which consumed his heart, and made it capable of the very severe sacrifice of martyrdom. It is the joy and the delight of the saints to suffer and die for God, and to see themselves become a victim united to Jesus Christ's sacrifice.

I think that if I had the honor of seeing you I would not recognize you, you have made so much progress in the ways of grace. I would

4. Mt 8:22; 1 Cor 15:28.

find that you are no longer among creatures, but in God, where you have withdrawn, to converse interiorly with Him, as in a Heaven, where the three Persons of the august Trinity dwell unceasingly, and are making your paradise there. On earth it is the life of pure faith which places you into that blessed abode; I call it the precursor to the life of glory.

If you are there, I rejoice infinitely more in that happiness than to see you sated with all earth's riches, which in all their greatness are nothing but a vapor and affliction of spirit.[5] However, in God, to serve is to reign and to be above all the misfortunes of the times. "Gustate et videte quoniam suavis est Dominus." Ps. 33:9.

n. 2439

Thanks for a relic which she gave

It was indeed my intention to render your dear person my very humble thanks today, for the precious treasure which we possess by your authority.[6] I hope that you will come to visit this holy relic which, on entering this house, filled the whole community with a wholly extraordinary joy. It is an immensely great consolation to possess such a rare trust. I am certain that your soul will receive great graces. We will ask this Saint to share with you the great love she had for God and that you may walk in the footsteps of her excellent virtues. My God, how lovable the saints are! Happy are the souls who aspire to sanctity, who forget creatures to remember the Creator, and who are separated from the earth to converse in heaven. May God grant me the favor of seeing you there.

I embrace your feet and wish you a good night.

n. 225

5. Cf. Eccl 1:14.

6. In 1660 the Duchess of Orléans made a gift to Mother Mectilde of the complete remains of St. Ida of Lorraine. The relics were found in the abandoned church of St.-Waast, a few kilometers from Boulogne-sur-Mer. At the time of the Revolution, the bones of St. Ida were transported to their monastery in Bayeux, where they are still venerated. Cf. Hervin, *Vie de Mere Mectilde*, 400 and also *Catherine de Bar: Documents Historiques*, 109.

Abandonment and Trust

Abandonment and trust in God

Oh, how good God is, how He is adorable and all love for you! Through these events see that He does not treat you like the great ones of the earth, but as the beloved of His heart and as one of those He has chosen on earth to honor the dispositions of His Son by state. Oh! How truly you said that God is rousing your faith by this most recent blow which His holy Providence is sending you.

I am delighted to see the sentiments which divine grace is pouring into your heart. You see the care that Our Lord takes to draw you into His holiness. He is separating you from the support of creatures, so that you find in Him alone the aid you need. Oh, the beautiful and heavenly words which you spoke with all your heart and which you express in your dear letter, "My Father who is in heaven." Say them often with faith and loving confidence, you will feel wonderful effects from it, and you will experience that He is truly your Father, your Spouse, and your All. It is not my prayers which won for your soul such strength and blessings. It is because your faith has been renewed and God is granting you the grace of making good use of your affliction, by receiving it from His adorable hand and submitting to His good pleasure. I entreat you, my dearest, continue to abandon yourself completely to Jesus Christ. Preserve the graces that He gives you and never more depend upon or make any creature a support. The one for whom God is not enough is too greedy. Here is your motto, goodbye to everything else; it is not worth a sigh from your good heart which should be consumed in the flames of pure love, as a perfect holocaust in an odor of sweetness.[1]

With regard to the request that you are making to God, I do not

1. Num 29:36.

know what spirit is urging you. I am a sinner and too much opposed to the holiness to which God is attracting you. I fear to create an obstacle to your soul. Still as it is an outpouring of your deep humility and your love for solitude, if your kindness were to permit me to be at your feet [to discuss it], I confess I would have the deepest joy in the world, in which I can find nothing pleasing except to be entirely God's and at your service.

n. 2422

We must consider distressing events in God's light
I asked God at Holy Communion that you will be able to make a holy use of the griefs you are enduring concerning this matter. In truth, it is a very trying thing according to the world's way of thinking, but it is necessary to consider it in an unworldly way.

Faith teaches us that both good things and bad things, except sin, come from God. You must adore His ways and find the grace to be consoled in His will. You will not have much difficulty in turning to God to find in Him the strength to bear these troubles, because of the long habituation you have had in bearing a hundred upsets, all the time. However, young N. who is not well versed in this practice will still have some difficulties in coming to terms with this. I beg and pray Our Lord to console him. Oh! A spiritually-minded soul like yours will draw excellent lessons from this misfortune! May it teach such a soul that we must not put our trust in man, and that the flatteries of those who have worldly power are normally without effect, "Nolite confidere in principibus."[2] However, we can say the opposite with regard to God's supreme majesty. The greater your faith and trust in Him, the more excellent are His gifts. Once and for all be convinced that the world does not hold anything but empty shows and semblances.

As for you, hide in Jesus Christ, since baptism buries you with Him, as St. Paul assures you when he says, "You are dead and your life is hidden with Jesus Christ in God."[3] How blessed is a soul to be no longer in the world and to have no support except in Him and to

2. Ps 145:2.
3. Col 3:3.

leave the dead to bury the dead! Courage! Do not be anxious, but say to God with Jesus Christ, "Non mea, sed tua fiat voluntas."[4] Do not lose your inner peace for anything, and after having done what you could do, say with the prophet, "Nisi Dominus aedificaverit domum in vanum laboraverunt qui aedificant eam."[5] And meanwhile, it is necessary to find it good that God is bringing us to nothingness in the manner He pleases. Console those who are grieved; but for yourself, remember that Our Lord is calling you to holiness and that you must find all your consolation in God. There is scarcely any for you in creatures, yet you will find it fully in Jesus Christ. In Him I am yours, with profound respect...

n. 686

On the uncertainty of life

A heart as firm as yours is needed in order not to be perturbed about such sudden and surprising events from divine Providence. A heart which is truly united to God is unshakable, and I will be overjoyed if yours is in that condition. This does not prevent a person from making a little reflection on the brevity of life and the uncertainty of the times. Our Lord says that He will come like a thief, by surprise, to oblige us to be on our guard and remain ready to depart. This is the best disposition for a beautiful soul who lives in a holy detachment. Knowing that she is in exile here, nothing keeps her on the earth; also knowing that Heaven is her Father's house and her eternal palace. She should long constantly for it, and ask to return there, as the prophet king did.[6] What we see happen to others can happen to us, and blessed is the soul whom the Lord will find watching. This is the deepest desire that I have for you, in which I am, with all the profound respects that I owe...

n. 552

How one must live and love God on earth

How the honor of your memory has a marvelous sweetness for me! I hope that Thursday, if the weather is good, you will do us the favor

4. Mk 14:36.
5. Ps 126:1.
6. Ps 26:4.

of coming to be diverted here by speaking about the One who is your heart's delight, and whom you love so perfectly. Oh! How good it is to speak of that adorable subject which constitutes the saints' happiness! Come, Madam, come, to delight in a holy manner in the mercies of Jesus. This conversation will relieve your fatigue and will increase His love in your soul. Let us learn how we must know and love the one whom we shall love for all eternity.

In fact, it is Jesus alone who can console the heart and give it a true joy. Everything created is nothing. Alas, the world is a place of malediction! It is a foreign land to God's children who mourn at the sight of their exile. My God, when will we leave this horrible captivity? Let us long for our fatherland. A child is permitted to desire to return to his father's house and to regret the delay. The prophet asked God, quite earnestly, to remain in His house all the days of his life. Now, there are three dwellings or mansions of God: Heaven, the church, and the depth of the Christian soul. We must hope to one day go to heaven never to leave it. We cannot always remain in the church; but we must try to never leave the depth of our souls, since God Three and One dwells there continually. There the soul should make a firm and stable abode, and there it will find heaven on earth. I pray Our Lord to draw you there sweetly and powerfully in such a way that you can find the rest, strength, and joy that I desire for you.

n. 446

How necessary it is to withdraw from the world

I leave you to judge whether or not the courier caused me to fear. Seeing him come so quickly gave me reason to think that some new affliction had befallen you, knowing that our Good God does not allow one little moment of your life to not be filled with His cross. That is the royal road by which you must travel. If you follow my advice, you should not look for any other. This is the way of His lovable Providence with regard to your soul. You must adore Him and submit blindly to it, because Our Lord wants you to have peace of soul through solitude, separating yourself completely [from the world].

I am more convinced than ever that you should withdraw with Jesus Christ, and bring to a close the troubled life which you have led this long while. In order to prepare you for this, I will tell you honestly that you should hope for nothing, either from this side or from that, from the elder or the younger. Seek and find your repose by yourself and hope in God alone. You must not hope in creatures. Always consider God, His glory, your salvation, and that of Miss N… You must put these before everything else that passes and is nothing but trifles. Eternity must have the victory over time, and God over creatures, which are mere nothings.

Continue your solicitations in Rome for the office of the Most Sacred Heart.[7] Meanwhile, we will pray for you to God to make known His most holy will. You must consult Him and then follow constantly what He will have shown you. For my part, I have a deep desire to see you at peace about this subject. All my zeal, after God's glory, is to draw down from heaven on you, and all that affects you, the abundance of blessings that I desire for you, and which you need in order to be a pure victim for the divine love. In Him, I am all yours, with profound respect…

n. 1763

The manner of abandoning oneself to God

I come from Holy Communion where you were so present before Our Lord that I cannot prevent myself from writing to you about the inspiration I received for you.

It seemed to me that the soul of Jesus was lamenting that your faith and abandonment towards His mercy were not complete, and that He desired from you a handing over of your whole self to Him; and that He wanted to take a paternal care of you and of everything that relates to you; and that if you could wisely leave your whole self to Him and to the care of His loving Providence, you would see the marvels of His goodness. Do this, then, with all your heart, rather than stopping short at your thoughts and reflections full of anguish and sorrow. For a long time I have begged you very insistently to do this. You must not put it off. Jesus's holiness desires to work in your soul; that is why it must be detached from its own thoughts, so as to

7. The Office of the Most Sacred Heart of Mary, composed by St. John Eudes, was published in 1648.

61

cleave firmly to His love. Let us live only from that love which transforms us completely in Jesus.

I have a great desire to be at your feet to speak about this, and
through this sweet conversation to chase away your weariness.
Courage! Continue the quarter of an hour with more attention than
ever.

n. 1576

A little spiritual medicine

I cannot wait until this evening to send word to know about your
health and if your syrup has benefited you. I want this very much,
but I do not know if it will have the power to purge and clear the
humor which is causing the vapors. I think you must add a certain
medicine which is not found at the apothecary's shop; you must get
it from the Heart of Jesus. [This medicine] is a lack of worry about
all that is not God, a dram of abandonment to His love, with a scruple[8] of holy indifference to all God's action. These produce a marvelous calm and serenity.

Madam, permit me to tell you something which affection cannot
restrain, with no lack of respect: that there is no means to break the
cord which ties my heart with yours in Jesus. Pardon my liberty
which is too great, which love cannot hide, although I try to enclose
it in Jesus Christ in order to purify it in Him, and to have no affection for you apart from Him, knowing well that you would not wish
for a purely natural affection, because you cannot be satisfied with
the friendship a subject owes to his sovereign; but one that is pure,
holy, and heavenly, and that comes from heaven in order to return
there. And I dare to assure you that it is, and that having taken root
in the Heart of Jesus, it is no less strong and unbreakable. Worldly
friendship is a straw which is burnt up at the first spark of a small
conflict, but nothing human can break the holy love which has its
source in God. The bond between our hearts is of this kind. It is
Our Lord who united them; flesh and blood have no part in it, that
is why it will be unbreakable and last eternally.

8. The dram is equal to 1/8th of an ounce. The scruple is equal to 0.05 of an
ounce.

I hope for it from your kindness which desires to permit it and which will do me the justice of believing that I am, in a manner that only God understands, all yours.

n. 1096

We must remain in Jesus

I entreat you to let me know how you are doing, and if your heart continues to remain firm and united to Jesus Christ, to be but one soul, one love, and one sacrifice with Him. If your will is not separated from Him, you will always find a secret strength and an inner grace in the depth of your heart which will bear everything. I do not doubt His protection. Madam, keep your soul calm through God, and you will do this easily if you remain in Jesus, whom you received this morning. I felt a very great joy about this. In a firm and gentle manner, try to put yourself above the objects of earth. You are a citizen of heaven; therefore, be an angel of Paradise by living only from Jesus, in Jesus, and for Jesus. In His love, I am all yours.

n. 1778

In adversity we must be submissive to God

Yesterday I was so displeased with you that I did not dare to write to you for fear of being disrespectful. The reason I was upset was that you are causing and hastening your death through your grief which you do not fight enough, not considering things from the side of God and His Providence; allowing yourself to be overwhelmed, which cannot be done without imperfection. You will have the kindness to allow me to reprimand you about this and tell you, with as much respect as zeal for your holiness, that you are not doing what God wants, by allowing yourself to be affected so much by things which distress the soul and are contrary to your desires.

You must have a little more abandonment to God, more submission to His ways, and faith in His goodness, otherwise you will not be doing what He wills. I beseech you to think about this. It is a little lesson that I am taking the liberty of giving you, in the most cordial fashion, but on the condition that you work at it gently and without anxiety. Do you want to render God's graces fruitless in your soul and neglect the means He is giving you to become a great saint? It is time to render God's intentions effective in you. He wants you to be completely His; but in love and through the path of love, and not through sadness and fear, which is the ruin of pure love, and which it drives from a heart when we give it admittance. Surely, if the Novice would believe the Novice Mistress, she would quickly leave her griefs and would experience the joy of the Holy Spirit, and the peace of God's children who live in the secure faith and hope of Our Lord's sure promises which are infallible.

Would to God that we were able to keep that dear Novice close: we would not allow her to be overwhelmed by so many useless thoughts, and returns which are fruitless. Your experience should make you more reliant on God's good pleasure, and increase your faith without your peace being troubled for a moment. However, let us say that this dear Novice flees the Novice Mistress so as to not leave the pain and grief which are destroying her health and this is greatly upsetting those who honor and esteem her perfectly...

n. 1549

It is necessary to entrust and abandon oneself entirely to God

In the presence of Our Lord Jesus Christ my soul finds itself entirely filled with your concerns, which causes us to offer to God our humble prayers for your intentions, without ceasing. I am doing this in a very particular way for your sanctity. I cannot think of the action of divine Providence concerning your royal House, without believing that God intends to sanctify it, and that if He has deprived it of glory and peace on earth, overturning it as with that of the holy man Job, He will raise it one day in Heaven more gloriously. Further, what consoles me in all these distressing events is to see your House raised in a holy way above all things, to prize nothing but the possession of God.

Oh! How blessed you are since you can remain firm amid all the tempests of this stormy sea, in the holy abandonment of your whole self to God. In this confidence and in this admirable faith you will experience peace and tranquility, while creatures are lost and consumed in the troubles of human life.

I humbly beseech you to remain as detached as you can interiorly, to preserve and maintain your soul in holy liberty, through which you will enjoy the sweet and loving union with God in a very easy way. You will experience His infinite goodness and the care that He will take for the success of your affairs. You will see that He will do more in one hour than all men with their industry and eagerness. It is a very high grace He is giving you which is causing you to make light of the things of this world. This disposition keeps you separate from corruption; thus you do not belong to the world. You are God's, created for God, coming from God, and strictly obliged to return to God. You must give Him every moment of your life. Madam, I am asking Him to draw you to Himself so powerfully, by the sacred bonds of His divine love, that you are entirely set aflame, and that you may glorify Him for all eternity with the blessed.

This is the most fervent desire of my heart for you, with which I am, with deep respect...

n. 2187

We must remain before God in the abyss of our nothingness

I cannot wait for the favor of your letters, since I am worried about your well-being. I think that my most frequent solicitations, after Jesus Christ and His most holy Mother, are to your most honored self; even at night I think of you.

We are praying and adoring God together for your affairs, your interests being mine: and if I dare to speak as to a common person, I would say it is in Jesus, and through Jesus, that these close ties between us have been made; but I am not speaking to you in this way, I would be too bold. It is enough to say that Our Lord does what He pleases and how it pleases Him. I know that I am nothing and I never lose sight of my nothingness and the sentiment of my unworthiness; it is what keeps me before God who knows everything and that is enough for me; He knows what He impressed on me for you. When I am truly God's you will experience how I am yours in His love and in His heavenly Spirit.

Take courage and place yourself in God, in His good pleasure. Adore the actions of His gracious Providence, which is delaying the happy moment of your precious solitude. Let us try to do this in the center and depth of our hearts, waiting until we can flee from creatures to go and bury ourselves fully alive; where we shall have no other occupation than to love and contemplate the one who must be the eternal object of our love and our felicity. Oh Madam, a little bread and a glass of water suffices to make a soul perfectly happy when it has God! Oh! When will we be in that blessed dwelling where God alone will be our only life? Outside of it there is only weariness, sighs, and tears. The heart of man cannot be satisfied except with God, and when it is deprived of that delightful possession, it feels only bitterness. That is the reward we receive amid the trouble of creatures, if our soul does not have the holy habit of withdrawing into God, leaving everything created in nothingness so as to remain hidden in Jesus Christ with God. If we do not learn to make this sweet retreat we will be in danger of being frequently troubled by life's contradictions, which are usually unavoidable. It is impossible to pass through life in repose among so many trying vicissitudes if we do not turn to God and find refuge in Him.

That is what you are trying to do, Madam, and what I ask Our Lord to accomplish in you through His grace and His love. Pardon my boldness, it is without leaving the profound respect with which I am...

n. 1097

God is changeless

If I had the gift of agility, I would come often to you to learn about your health. Set aside every grief, forget everything, and ignore creatures. Oh! How good it is to be God's; He does not change at all and is always Himself. You know it through the experience which you continually have of it.

Remain firm and resolutely attached to His goodness, with an unshakable confidence—whoever has God has everything—and whoever desires only His most holy will finds peace and joy everywhere. I cannot prevent myself from wanting to be at your feet to declare to you that I am yours without any reserve, with respect...

n. 2682

On patience and conformity to God

Provided that I am reassured about your health, that is enough for me. This note is to ask you: not wanting to pester you but only to assure your dear person that I am thinking of your troubles and of the means to deliver you from them. I hope for this from the One for whom nothing is impossible and who cannot reject the soul who trusts itself completely to Him, as you are trying to do. You must persevere in this and say with the holy man Job, "Though He should kill me yet I would hope in His goodness."[9] This is the living and lively faith which moves mountains, and which works miracles. It is by this pure faith that the righteous should live, and by which you should act, since you are written in the book of life and are in the precious number of the predestined. Rejoice in that loving confidence; your pains will end one day and joy and eternal repose will follow forever, and this will be soon. Courage! Let us suffer with love in this beautiful hope which gave such strength and courage to martyrs, and made them sing joyfully in the midst of the flames and of their extremely violent ordeal, "Dominus illuminatio mea et salus mea. Quem timebo? Dominus protector vitae meae quid trepidabo?"[10] What can we fear when God is our protector, our light, and our salvation?

n. 2510

The will of God constitutes all things

Madam, by His action, Our Lord is showing your soul that He takes more pleasure in your adoring Him on the cross than on the altar today. That is why He makes you unable to come to the poor little house and solitude of the Blessed Sacrament. You must love His holy will and be sacrificed to His good pleasure. In whatever state His gracious Providence places us, let us serve Him in His fashion, and not according to our inclinations. All the ups and downs which ruin our plans give us the means to die to our desires, by continually sacrificing our little projects. I think you do this often. Likewise, occasions for this are not lacking to your person. We must try to bless God in everything, and accustom ourselves meekly to His actions. This is the way He acts to perfect his elect. I am entering

9. Job 13:15.
10. Ps 26:1–3.

into the same disposition with you regarding this, enduring the privation of your dear self since He wills it, which [privation] is the one most deeply felt to me in the world. I ask Him with all my heart that your malady will not grow worse. I am going to pray to Our Lord for this purpose.

n. 2294

The soul united to God is incapable of change

I was very consoled yesterday in the evening by the letter with which you were pleased to honor me. The holy resolution to be more and more God's than ever gave joy to my poor heart. I am certain that if you are faithful, half of your troubles will be consumed in God by the pure flames of His love, almost without your feeling it. But you must hold firm a little, if you want to be delivered from the thousand small bitter things that the vicissitudes life bring all the time. We must defend ourselves from them, by remaining firmly attached to God, by a living faith, adoring His divine immutability, which makes Him always the same in Himself, and incapable of any change. The soul who lives from God, in God, participating in His adorable qualities, becomes immutable, remaining intimately united to God, saying with the Prophet, "What do I desire in heaven or on earth? Nothing except you my God."[11]

I know that the world has nothing lovable and that it has no charm to hold you; you do not want to have any part of it. But although we do not love it, it does not cease causing a thousand reasons for anxiety for you if we do not remain hidden in Jesus Christ, in God. We must try to never leave Him, so that human things do not separate us from our loving union with God, which the devil cannot bear.

I await your news with confidence in the mercy of God for which we pray without ceasing...

n. 978[12]

11. Ps 72:25.
12. Presented following the manuscript DR, 669.

Allow Jesus to reign; God alone

I received a great joy yesterday evening, when I learned through the letter with which you honored me that your health is better and that we will have the honor of seeing you tomorrow. I will put aside everything and will say my *Paternosters* in the morning, in order to have great leisure. Oh! It is such a long time since I have had this favor! I am impatient, and I learn that the bad weather played me a trick, preventing you from writing to me. For many years I have experienced that what I desire with great fervor, Providence does not give me. If I had less affection, I would be less eager, but I do not lose hope. If you have many things to tell us, so do I on my part. If Providence put me in a corner at your feet we would speak of God at our ease, and we would learn the means to do His gracious will, and to be occupied with Him alone. O blessed life which is spent from God, in God, and for God! It is not filled with bitterness like life in the world; it shares in the peace of paradise and the joy of the Holy Spirit. He is in the depth of the soul and heart, and in love produces what cannot be expressed, but which is sweeter than all the delights of earth. Therefore, let us hasten to love the One who is so uniquely lovable. I beseech you most humbly to love and adore Him for me.

n. 763[13]

Exhortation to patience

Your precious letter breaks my heart. My God, how the conduct of men is different from that of God! When will it happen that His divine Spirit will be our guide and creatures will no longer make difficulties? Madam, take courage, I promise you that God will take a very special care of you and of all your dealings. Make a firm resolution to do what God asks of you, and try to understand it according to the simplicity of grace. When we do what we can, He does not ask for more. I pray Him to draw you beyond creatures and to bind and attach you completely to Himself; and you will see that peace will be established in your heart and you will enjoy paradise on

13. Presented according to manuscript DR, 763.

earth. I wish it for you with the same heart with which I am, with profound respect...

n. 2958[14]

Go to God and benefit from His love

Providence did not give me one little moment of time yesterday to finish the letter that I began to write to you after Matins. I was mortified about this. My spirit is often at your feet, Madam, and I think often of your affairs, more than of my own. Your salvation is precious to me, but my wish is that you would tend generously toward holy perfection since Our Lord tells us, "Be perfect, as your Father in heaven is perfect."[15] Madam, I beg you humbly to work at this and to begin earnestly this Lent to go to God, and benefit from His love. We will speak of this again on Thursday if you come to the exposition of the Blessed Sacrament.

n. 1912

Mectilde tells of the pleasure she takes in writing to the Duchess

If I followed my inclination, you would be bothered by my letters too often; but I make many sacrifices which deprive me of this consolation, knowing that I can say nothing which is capable of giving you joy except speaking of Him who is the felicity of the saints, whose number you will one day increase.

On Saturday I wanted to write you something on this subject, although I am unworthy; but remembering that good Father N. could speak to you about this enchanting subject more effectively than I could, I left him that commission, thinking that he will open it for you. I see ineffable mysteries in the action that God is taking concerning your soul. If you reflect a little about this, you will see clearly that your heart should be completely detached from earth, and that it should be so completely given to God that you are only on earth by His command. You must make room for the spirit of Jesus which wants to dwell in the depth of your soul. If you can

---

14. From MS P110; the following letters are all taken from this manuscript.
15. Mt 5:48.

allow it do so, you will see how He will lead you in the paths of holiness: this is your vocation. He commands you to aspire to it when He says, "Be holy, because I am holy."[16] One must not fear that this commandment lacks grace and the means to attain it; since Our Lord desires our sanctification infinitely, He will give us everything we need to be sanctified. Let us begin to be faithful in corresponding to God's designs regarding ourselves: we cannot go back. I believe that you desire this with all your heart. The little book about contemplation will lead you straight to God in order to rest in His Sacred Heart. Now, the Heart of God is nothing other than the divine will, but in a manner completely full of love and trust: "*Gustate et videte quoniam suavis est Dominus.*"[17]

We expected the Guardian to know if he chooses to lodge Fr. N.[18] However, in the name of God, before making a decision, consider before God if Our Lord puts unction into his words to lift your soul in the love of our Divine Savior. I wait on your will.

Do not be anxious; preserve your interior peace and the holy liberty which Our Lord gave you, and try to love Him with a pure love before you die.

n. 2689

Regarding her continual crosses

I read the letter from Father N., in which I see almost always the same thing. I mean, those letters are always seasoned with the taste of the cross. You receive scarcely anything from that side which does not have this character. You would be overwhelmed if you became accustomed to digesting such morsels! But thanks be to God, you are the Strong Woman of which Scripture speaks.[19] You are not troubled about what men say or do. You have fixed the anchor of your hope in God; nothing can shake you.

16. Lev 11:45; 1 Pet 1:16.
17. Ps 34:8.
18. The Father Guardian: superior of a convent of Friars Minor from the Order of St. Francis.
19. Proverbs 31.

God is! This is a great truth, one which gives a marvelous consolation to faithful souls who take their rest in Him and expect everything from His goodness. Do not lose your repose, do not alter your peace. God is, and that is to say everything to the one who can understand. It is not only that He is in Himself, but He is in you; He is with you; He is for you. He is in you to sustain and animate your being; He is with you to act and work; He is for you to protect and defend you. He is your light, He is your guidance, He is your strength and your virtue.

Yet He is [also] your Father. If you dwell in Him, He will dwell in you. Therefore, believe with a faith which is certain and does not waver that He takes a particular care of everything that affects you; that He not only thinks of sanctifying you, but that He knows even a hair on your head, which does not fall without His permission. Oh, if our heavenly Father takes care of such a small thing, will He not take care of all the rest? And if you can put everything into His divine hands, what will He not do on behalf of a soul if it entrusts itself to Him in the right fashion, without many thoughts about His creature's unworthiness? Alas, He knows well that man is a sinner and nevertheless He does not refuse His aid. No one who is not abandoned wholly into His hands, delivering every concern to His loving Providence, knows by experience God's mercies. Where is the person who has trusted in Him and been confounded?[20] Where human means fail, His power will not fail, if His infinite wisdom judges that things are useful for His glory and for the salvation of His creatures.

It is here that you may stir up an entirely divine faith, based on God's mercies, on His infallibility in His works and His love in His actions concerning you and what affects you. Strip yourself as much as possible of human views; attach yourself to the good pleasure of God alone so that the troubles of life do not disturb the tranquility of your heart. Always view things as God views them, wanting them only for Him, doing them only for Him, finding life only in Him. In the midst of your difficulties, do not lose the moments for your

20. Cf. Ps 34:5.

sanctity. Go straight to God, without turning to the right or the left. God is enough for the soul who knows how to love. Love and think of God, and God will think of you and your affairs for you.

n. 708

The special graces of a good soul

Madam, I fear that the great heat will prevent your coming, which gives me the honor of writing you this message that there is no treaty about what we suspected. God sees all; we must put every-thing into His holy hands. When you have done all that you can, you must expect the success you desire from on high, and mean-while leave everything to God, seeing all things in the action of His Providence, directed by His divine wisdom. Enter into God and be strengthened in His love; without waiting any longer, use the time to become more and more holy.

The good soul, about whom I spoke, will come here one of the days of our holy octave, the one that will please you, in order to have the honor of paying her respects to you. She honors you all the more since she regards you as one predestined. I can assure you that this person is not ordinary with regard to the elevation of grace. However, since she does not want her degree of union with God to be known, she remains very little and detached and without any affectation. I would be very glad for you to meet her. She will obtain for you many blessings from heaven, since I am certain she is very powerful: she has sublime gifts, even prophecy. But in the name of God, she must not know what I am telling you about her. You must leave her in God until He manifests her. I assure your piety that she prays to God for you in the proper way.

n. 929

Regarding submission to God's will

I do not know if we ought to rejoice about the news that was just brought to me. I am asking God to bring about His glory from it. One must bless Him for everything and say with the heart and the mouth, "*Fiat voluntas tua.*"

God's actions are so wondrous that often creatures cannot under-stand them at all. We must submit to them blindly and try not to lose peace and tranquility of soul. It is better to possess the grace and love of Jesus than to gain all the empires of the world. We must die and lose everything to obtain heaven. Crosses, sufferings, insults, etc., serve as currency to purchase it. You have the advantage of sharing in them sufficiently to obtain it. Courage, Madam, your woes will not prevent you from becoming a great saint, sacrificing yourself as a victim of love to God's good pleasure.

In this humble disposition you will find the sure remedy for your woes and your soul will be perfected in an exceptional way. God loves you too much to leave you without suffering, since it is the wood and raw material which keeps the fire of His divine love alight in your heart. If you do not see the flames, it is because the ash of nature's little aversions covers them. They do not prevent it from burning imperceptibly and consuming the thousand inclinations of pride, which finds itself so often in captivity. Pride groans under the weight of God's powerful hand which is crushing it in this way, through everything that seems to me to be divine mercies for you.

God wants to make you holy and I am begging Him to give you the grace necessary to correspond to this, so that by losing creatures every day, you will find the Creator more easily and fully. Madam, I know that this is your only desire, and the happiness for which your soul longs, since you are fully persuaded that it is only God who can satisfy and fulfill it. In truth, all the rest is not worth a thought, or one moment of anxiety, whatever upheaval may happen.[21]

On Thursday we were sorry not to see you at the little house of the Blessed Sacrament. At the foot of the holy altar, Madam, you receive a divine strength, one able to make you conquer everything, and to keep your heart detached from all things, to abide in God alone, and to live in Him by His pure love. I pray Him to govern your being so powerfully that it may be living and animated through His Spirit. This is the fervent desire of...

n. 1192

21. Manuscript P100 ends here. There, the last paragraph is a separate note. Manuscripts T11 and P121 make one single letter of these two texts.

Regarding depression or reducing grief

It will be impossible for you to keep on much longer if you are going to let your afflictions weigh you down so. Our Lord wills that your soul should rise above everything around you, that you attach yourself gently to God; that you possess Him, in faith, within your-self, without looking for Him any longer, and that He wants you to be renewed in His Spirit. Your suffering nature, which, I see, has almost no vigor, needs to make a little effort. It mustn't happen that so excellent a victim is consumed in any fire other than that of pure and divine love; this would be to fall short of God's designs con-cerning your soul. Your soul cannot ignore that it is being led by the gentleness and love that make one rest in God through a simple surrender of all that you are to His holy Providence, abandoning everything to Him, so that it will not be anxious about anything anymore.

I know well that this practice is quite difficult for a quick mind [like yours] which, having understood, sees in a moment more than what the most enlightened people could say. I admit this, but one needs to simplify, or at least put aside, what the mind sees, and should there be no remedy, one must surrender oneself to God's goodness with a humble resignation and with confidence.

I am certain that, if we but had a little more faith, we would often see miracles in the things that concern us, but the greatest of these would be peace and tranquility in our inmost being. I have a burn-ing desire that you come to have that condition, and that you may be so intimately united to Jesus that you will be unshakable in the midst of the vicissitudes of this life, which consists of nothing but vanity, inconstancy, and affliction of spirit. This is why one must hold things in a passing way, making use of them as if not using them, remaining free in the midst of cares, relying on this infallible truth: God is.

I have humbly begged you to spend a quarter of an hour each day on this truth, pondering it in faith. This is how to do it: at the most free and convenient hour of the day you must shut yourself up in a little room where, kneeling down, or seated if you cannot do other-wise, by a simple act of faith in God, you believe Him present in your innermost soul, believing in Him in all His attributes and divine perfections, without making distinctions. You can say, "My God, You are. I believe that You are what You are, and I believe myself to be a pure nothing in your holy Presence." After these words, or others that the Holy Spirit inspires, you must remain in silence, in a profound respect before that infinite greatness, humbling yourself profoundly, leaving aside every [mental] operation, reasoning, and consideration, to let yourself sink into this adorable All. You have to restrain the acts of your mind during this quarter of an hour, so as to feel only the delicate touches of the Holy Spirit in your inmost heart. Don't think this a waste of time; if you are faithful to it, you will see that this [kind of] prayer contains an inexhaustible treasury of grace. As beginnings are a little difficult, you will only do a quarter of an hour, but do this without fail. If you give me the pleasure of coming to see me, we will talk about it more specifically.

Let us learn to live here below as the saints live in heaven, and practice doing on earth what we hope to do for all eternity. Let us love, adore, and possess within ourselves the same God who is the glory and happiness of the blessed. Amen.

n. 215

Here is the letter to Father... I return it to you and wish you good day, filled with as many blessings as I wish for myself, but above all with a fervent love for Jesus Christ. This is what I ask for you so that, by the adorable operations of that divine fire, your soul may be raised in such a way to God that it is inaccessible to all earthly things, but particularly those which can cause you unhappiness. Surely, it is only a heart united with God that can endure the bitterness of life without dejection. In this life, we cannot live without contradictions. Divine Providence even joins in to furnish occasions for this, but if we can adore the hand that wounds us, we will find the good in the midst of the evils and life in death. For this, we must remain united to Jesus and not want anything except the good pleasure of His Father, just as He willed only His holy will.

Madam, always see yourself as a little ball of wax in the hand of God, to be formed according as He pleases. Be without choice and without desire, so that you can receive the operations of His pure love. Do not put anything of yourself in you, but leave yourself completely, without any reserve, without fear, and without reflection to the one who has more kindness for you than you could ever have for yourself. Live by faith, confidence, and love. That is the path of grace in you and the intention of God regarding you. Your humility is allowing me to speak to you in this way.

n. 2933

I write to wish you good day and ask about the state of your illness. May God will everything to be better than it was yesterday. The whole community goes to Communion for your health, asking it of God through Jesus Christ and the intercession of His most holy Mother; and for Him to give you all the graces you need and especially a loving confidence and an unshakable peace. This is the fruit of the Holy Spirit; when a soul possesses this it experiences its effects, which are wondrous. I ask Him to complete in you the sanctity which He has so well begun, perfecting that great multitude of graces He has granted you from your childhood, and which you have happily preserved amid the world's corruption.

You have the mark of the predestined, that is quite true; but persevere, since you know that the one who does not advance retreats. Now, in pursuing Christian perfection, we must never cease to tend toward God with our whole heart, to submit to His good pleasure, and to hope, through His holy mercy, that He will do by His grace what we cannot do, although we have good will. We must love our dependence on a goodness so unutterable and which loves us with an infinite love. Without faith and trust we never experience the holy effects of that love, know His loving guidance or the paternal care of His loving Providence. The soul must be completely surrendered to God and expect everything from His kindness; it should be concerned about nothing except pleasing Him. Such a soul would see in the future what my pen is not able to express, but what God's good and faithful servants taste and experience. I desire all these precious blessings for you.

n. 1618

If the Novice Mistress dared, she would impose a penance on the dear Novice every time she thought that she is a burden to her and that, under this pretext, kept back all the sorrows and bitterness of her soul in her heart. The Novice Mistress is not ignorant of the great mark of friendship that trust is, but she does not ask for anything more than what can console her dear Novice. There are things that can be said without consequence and which are reasons for our sorrow nonetheless. Why hold them back since the future makes them known, and this Novice could lessen the anguish of her heart by speaking about them? When the wound is uncovered, the evil is half cured—at least it is not so dangerous. I know that it is not a lack of confidence, although the Novice Mistress is unworthy; rather it is that the Novice becomes discouraged by herself and finds consolation in nothing. It is also true that nothing human is capable of consoling her; but the things of God can strengthen and encourage her to endure the crosses that are in the order of God's good pleasure. One must do a little violence to oneself and the impossible becomes easy; with grace we can do everything. I am holding back my thoughts so that I do not reprimand the dear Novice too strictly. But I beseech her very humbly to come and see the Novice Mistress if she does not want to undergo a little correction. If she delays she will forget her lesson and what will become of the quarter of an hour? There has been no account of whether it is being done or not. Nevertheless I promised God to lead her gently into the Heart of Jesus Christ where she should find the life, the repose, and the joy that the world and creatures cannot give. If I take such a strong interest, if I keep her so close...

n. 2692

I thank God that your health is better; we are in great fear of losing you. As for me, I confess that I often cried many tears. Our Lord sees them, and I pray with all my heart that He is giving you all the graces that I ask for you, and above all that He will draw you to Holy Communion more frequently. Remember that all your strength and your holiness are in Jesus Christ and that He is the life of your soul. How can it live without receiving that divine life? In the name of God, try to Communicate more often: your health will be stronger, your soul more illuminated, your union with God will be more complete and the peace will make a heaven of your soul; apart from this there is only bitterness and pain. Let us go to God at every hour; let us honor His divine will in everything; let us leave creatures which draw us away from the pure love we owe God; let us learn to love Him perfectly in this world, since we must love Him in eternity. Oh! What regret to not have loved the one who is so uniquely lovable!

I pray that adorable Savior to hold you close in His love, and that all your happiness in this life may be to consume your being in its divine flames.

I wish you a good night and a full measure of the grace which will cause you to live only for Jesus Christ.

n. 903 *bis*

I hope to have the honor of embracing your feet before I go on retreat. I am deferring it again a few days in order to look after some little domestic affairs, and I will not hide myself away without receiving your commands. I assure you that if God hears my prayers, you will feel some benediction on account of my retreat. I intend to speak to God about all my concerns there, and especially about your sanctification, and the necessary means for you to attain the high perfection God wills for you. We must no longer waste time, it is too short and too precious: its price is the blood of Jesus Christ. He gives it to us in order to love Him: let us desire nothing more than Him and may your soul not cease seeking Him until you possess Him. It is necessary to lose oneself and be lost in Him. This is the good evening I wish you.

n. 1436

Madam, you cannot give me more joy than by assuring me of the improved health of your most honored person. I regard it as a gift from God in such a distressing time. From this I foresee a very good consequence for the future.

Madam, you say rightly that we must be entirely God's, without any more delay. Let us be converted every day, more and more completely to Him in the present moment. He awaits only our inward return. It is very easy for us, since we have Him in our souls and there is no need to go and seek Him in our churches for this. We have only to recollect ourselves interiorly, in faith, and adore Him in us with profound reverence. As soon as the soul is turned to Him by a simple and loving return, it finds Him through the movement of His grace, as if He said, "Here I am. Be Mine and I will be all yours." O word, which carries away the heart and which sometimes even enraptures the senses! To find a God so close to us, and in a manner so beyond words that it seems that He has nothing to do except give Himself completely to us and fill us with His graces!

Oh, what great and wonderful things happen in the heart of the just person, I mean, in a soul in a state of grace who acts through His Spirit! Alas, because we do not believe or feel Him, we are always seeking God and we do not find Him. That is because we are seeking outside of ourselves. However, He dwells in the depth of the soul and there He carries out the sweet and delightful operations of His love. Therefore, let us not seek Him in creatures, since the Gospel assures us the kingdom of God is within us. Let us not go elsewhere. Oh! How good it is to be in that ground of peace where we find God alone and where creatures and the world cannot disturb the peace we possess.

Madam, I fervently wish for your beautiful soul to find its refuge and repose in that little paradise amid the weariness and griefs of this sad life. I ask your guardian angel to lead you into it and that you may remain there always; you will experience in it what I cannot express. I am certain that even your body would be strengthened.

Pardon, Madam, this is just a little something to amuse you.

n. 3123

Madam, forgive a heart which has too much affection: friendship sometimes makes one depart from respect, and say what must not be thought. Forget that little outburst. When one possesses a good that one cannot deserve, one always fears to lose it. You have done me too many favors, your extreme kindness made me presumptuous, but today I am putting an end to all my self-love's outbursts.

The letter you did me the honor of writing me will be carefully kept, to cure such attacks at the first approach; it is a very strong remedy. I would to God we could discover a similar remedy for the vapors and the spleen pains which do not leave you in peace! I know what could relieve it: it is a remedy which requires a little courage, sacrificing to God the many little things that you can conquer, which are suffocating your poor heart. I see it at every hour almost ready to die and depart. If there is no help on earth, let us go to seek it in heaven. Madam, is it possible to see you in a continual death without feeling your sorrow? It is impossible, one's heart must burst, if I dare to use that term, to see you every day in agony. With all my strength I am asking God to uphold you. I hope that His omnipotence will do it and that He will flood your soul with an abundance of graces. I asked for this yesterday almost the whole day and for Him to dilate your heart in the sweetness of His divine love, to make you share in the joy of the saints. While waiting for Him to transfer you from this world to that of glory, we must take heart, with a holy hope of seeing you there one day. That is your fatherland; earth is a place of exile and banishment. However, through divine grace, we will leave it to go to our Father in heaven's house; this truth gives joy to the heart. I will continue my poor prayers for you and for all those close to you, although we can hope that they are now in glory and more at peace than we are.

Courage, Madam, let us go to God through paths that He pleases; provided we arrive at our blessed end, that is enough; all the rest will sooner or later be reduced to nothing. I pray Our Lord to strengthen you more and more, and to give you the grace to neglect nothing that you should do and not to be troubled about the bad results which sometimes follow our endeavors. God and nothing more. Pure abandonment draws down from heaven wonderful effects of divine protection; if you remain in it, all will go for you in benediction.

n. 2449

Madam, I welcome the letter it pleased you to honor me with. In reply, I am taking the liberty of telling you with confidence and respect that you are too perturbed about what is written to you, and that you should accustom yourself to receiving blows without being the slightest bit distressed and know once and for all that God takes care of His own affairs, and that we must be attached uniquely and immovably to Him. Those who make the most noise are not the ones who handle their affairs best. Madam, be certain that God is taking care of you and all that affects you. Do not decrease your trust. You are killing your body and your soul through so much grief, and cause me a pity and compassion which pierce my heart. I have an incomparable confidence in the most holy Heart of the Mother of Jesus. A little patience and you will see its fruits. I have a great desire to be at your feet, and I hope that this will be soon. I am having N. come and another here to set up a fine house of the Blessed Sacrament and that you might have the consolation of going there to withdraw.[22] Madam, it is the place where one must go to possess the repose of a sweet and tranquil solitude, which your piety has desired for so long. I hope always that I will have the honor to be part of that group; provided that I am at your feet it is enough for me. I hasten to possess that precious consolation.

n. 1340

I am asking permission of your dear and honored person to console me about the cross that Our Lord placed on my shoulders.[23] It seems to me that it would not be so deeply felt if I had the requisite qualities and necessary dispositions to manage it well. In my inadequacy I must bless God and remain completely abandoned to His good pleasure, begging Him with all my heart to take pity on His work. With good reason I fear that it will perish in my hands if your holy prayers do not obtain from heaven for me blessings to sustain it, Madam.

n. 965

22. If this refers to the convent in Toul, the letter would then be from 1664–1665; if it concerns the aggregation of the convent of Our Lady of Consolation in Nancy, it would be from 1668–1669.

23. According to P121 M, Mother Mectilde alludes here to her re-election as prioress of the monastery of Rue Cassette. We can date this note then to 1664 or 1667.

Madam, the cross was the victory of your holy patroness; that is why I am taking the liberty to present to you a little image of her, which shows that her thoughts and cares are in the cross of Jesus Christ. I add to it another miniature which is the image of the most holy Virgin, from whom you expect help and protection for the blessed governance of your life. We will beg that august Mother of love to pour out on you those graces with which her virginal heart is filled and that she place in yours as many sparks of pure love as are needed to make a divine fire. This is the very precious bouquet which I desire to present to you in honor of your feast day. Madam, the whole community is going to Communion for your holy intentions, and to ask Our Lord to enkindle you with the delightful flames which gloriously consume the saints in paradise.

n. 1840

On the feast of St. Margaret

The garden of the house of the Daughters of the Blessed Sacrament does not produce any flowers worthy of being given today to your Royal Highness. I would have been very displeased about this, my Lady, if I did not find in the Eucharistic flowerbed an admirable supplement; it is the flower of the field, the lily of the valleys, Jesus, the eternal Word, who makes Himself the ornament of pure souls.[24] Madam, I am giving you that divine floweret, which the whole Community received for your Royal Highness this morning, beseeching Him to produce in you all the virtues which would render your soul a precious *marguerite*[25] in the eyes of your heavenly Spouse, through constancy and generosity in sufferings, and in imitation of your holy patroness, who was not discouraged by the difficulties found in the life of grace—the life to which, Madam, you aspire unceasingly. This is what we asked of God for your Royal Highness and for N., who, I think, bears your name.[26] So, Madam, receive this bouquet from paradise: those of earth are too paltry for

---

24. Literally, *bouquet*—here, a small bouquet of flowers meant to be worn.
25. *Marguerite* can mean both daisy and pearl in French.
26. Maybe Marguerite-Louise, the eldest of her daughters.

a soul who can enjoy only the beauties of the adorable lily[27] whom you love so dearly, and whom you contemplate so sweetly on our altars. I beg Him fervently to draw you with His divine power, in the odor of His sacred and precious perfumes; and may your soul be so perfumed with them that everything on the earth is displeasing to it, and being animated with Jesus's life alone, it may one day be consumed in the flames of His holy love. This is the constant desire of those who have the honor to be, with deep respect, all of them, without reserve...

n. 1983[28]

We must esteem crosses more highly than raptures

I wonder at your kindness, Madam, when you took pains yesterday to honor me with your letters, relieving my fear and giving me some peace of mind, so I could pass the night more calmly, by assuring us of your improved health. Mr. N. assured us that we will have the honor of embracing your feet on the day of our great feast for certain. We are praying for you insistently.

While awaiting that favor, we will continue our little prayers with all possible zeal for your complete recovery and sanctification, knowing that you do not love life if it is not completely holy. Be holy, Madam, Our Lord desires this of you. He is giving you the means for it, of which the most excellent are sufferings; these you never lack. It remains only to make a holy use of them; this is what you are doing with all your heart, considering yourself fortunate to be conformed to our adorable, crucified Savior.

St. Paul made more of this grace than of his rapture to the third heaven. The whole felicity of holy souls is to be fixed to the cross with Jesus; you are of this number since you suffer almost unceasingly; He will crown your sufferings.

Take heart, I beseech you, and remain sure of His help and His heavenly blessings. I wish this for you in good measure while embracing your feet with profound respect.

n. 657

27. The lily is a royal symbol in France; referring to Jesus as a lily indicates His kingship.
28. This letter is taken from MS Sor, 216.

If you were grieved Thursday at not being able to assist at the Benediction of the Most Blessed Sacrament, I can assure you that I was, too, and more deeply, since I consider your dear person as the finest ornament of our choir and the object in which Our Lord Jesus Christ takes most delight. Whenever you are missing I am pained, feeling that the homage we render to God in this mystery of love is incomplete.

That is why, Madam, I am asking God with all my heart that the earthly Majesties do not prevent you again from coming to render your homage to the heavenly Majesty who dwells on the altar as on His Eucharistic throne, for [the purpose of receiving] your love and to draw you completely to Him. I hope that next Thursday you will repair this lack, although it is not your fault. You will experience His divine presence more sweetly and He will kindly console the one who has no greater felicity in the present life than to be at your feet, to admire God's mercies for your soul and the actions of His lovable Providence for your sanctification.

My Lady, I can say that God holds you in His divine hands and makes it felt, to those who offer their prayers to the Lord for you, that He is applying Himself so much to your soul that He desires to make it the storehouse of His delights and to draw you away from creatures. If my heart could express what it understands and God allowed you to have some sort of belief in it, you would find a singular joy at seeing how He is advancing His work; He is preparing you to lead you into a place of repose wherein no creature can interrupt your soul's peace and turn it aside for a moment from the one who is its life and its all. O, Madam, when shall we leave this exile to return to the heart of God our Father, from whom we have come? Madam, I guess that your heart has no more ardent desire, and I have no greater passion, than to follow you to that precious dwelling and to be at your feet; there I am bowing in spirit and with profound respect, I am...

n. 2719

Exhortation to leave the world

The precious lines you deigned to take the trouble to write yesterday for my consolation make me infinitely indebted to your kindness.

They cause me to take the liberty of telling you that I praise God with all my heart for the resolution of breaking your bonds He inspired you to make. Your health is so delicate that one cannot be certain about it humanly speaking: the accident which happened shows that nature has suffered a great blow. We must try to avoid such things as much as we can. I know of no more effective way of doing this than to withdraw from the world.

Madam, seek your rest and your sanctification, this is permitted to you.[29] We see in history that many great monarchs abandoned everything in order to have some years of solitude before death. We know of great prelates who, [though] seeming by their sacred ministry to be inseparably attached to the governance of the Church, also withdrew. In my opinion, it is a great grace to have a little time to think seriously about God and oneself. We must not depart from this world without loving Him, and to attain that heavenly science we must leave the turmoil of creatures as much as possible. It is not that we cannot love God in the houses of the great, but that since Our Lord is little known in such places, it is rare to find souls there who are truly filled with His divine love. We see also those who have some trace of it not remaining there, knowing that they could not preserve it themselves for long. Let us flee the world, let us flee creatures if we want to rejoice fully in God alone. We cannot possess Him completely if we do not distance ourselves from what is opposed to Him and robs us of Him.

Believe me, Madam, if you are at night [in spirit] in our cell, I am in spirit at your feet, accompanying you in your sufferings and encouraging you to bear them in a holy way. However, permit me to tell you, my Lady, that you desire to endure them in too generous a way in the depth of your heart, without taking a little solace. I know that this is suffering heroically, but also cruelly, if I dare to use that term, because your good heart, which wants to endure everything for God, through continual sacrifices is disturbing your poor nature

29. M. Mectilde is likely alluding to the Duchess's idea of retiring to the monastery of Our Lady of Consolation in Nancy, whether in 1660 after the death of her husband, or in 1668–69 when the monastery was aggregated to the Benedictines of Perpetual Adoration.

so much that it succumbs, and cannot withstand it. If your body were strong enough to do this, it would be good, but God does not want us to rush into the tomb. With all my affection I am asking Him to give you aid through some good person, to unburden your heart a little and that you may receive some consolation. I hope Our Lord will provide this. I know how precious your good soul is to Him and how His mercy is protecting you and preparing great blessings for you. You must think seriously about rebuilding your health and after that make a holy resolution before God. You can confer with the good Father J. who is a great servant of God and whom the Holy Spirit will enlighten. You can also add to your counsel Fr. N. who will soon be here and others whom you will trust. Finally, you must get through this in one fashion or another, because in an important matter an uncertain mind cannot be free of trouble.

n. 171

There is a wind rising with such force that I must give up hoping for the honor of your presence today. What causes me to trouble you with these lines is to tell you about the relapse of Fr. J. It was not to be expected [that he would recover], his health is too broken. We will be told that he went to Heaven. However, I would have liked him to advise you about what God desires of you concerning your complete sanctification. We must abandon ourselves without reserve to His adorable Providence: it will provide in this. I am glad you have resolved to make your devotions tomorrow: you need strength, light, and grace to continue advancing in perfection, not-withstanding life's trials. You will find in Jesus Christ everything you need. Receive Him, as often as you can, and say to Him with all your heart many times during the day, "My God what do you want me to do? My heart is ready for your holy will." Farewell, my Lady, you must become holy through your woes and always be prepared to suffer. We will have prayers said for this.

n. 2943

This note is to ask you for news of your health and to tell you that your interests and those of your daughters are in my heart. Madam, you know that I am all yours in Our Lord and more deeply than ever, that I have a very great desire for your sanctification, and that I wish to die for your salvation.

I beseech you, by the bowels of Jesus Christ's divine charity,[30] seriously to consider separating yourself from all that can create an obstacle to your perfection. Let us go to God in the right way, with trust and love. Make a firm resolution to put to rights anything which could trouble your soul. Do not wait until the moment when the ability to do so is taken away from you. We must not put off until death the good we have to do, and especially what could disturb our soul's peace. I am urged interiorly to entreat you to do what God and your conscience are asking of you, to grant you that sweet and tranquil repose which the Holy Spirit produces in a purified heart.

See what Our Lord is asking of you; listen to the voice of His love, which is telling you to be entirely His. Review your temporal condition and your debts to find the means to satisfy them; see if your alms are given according to order and charity, with the purity of intention which should render them worthy of God; see if you are not acting too humanly in some dealings, and if your kind heart is not pouring itself out too freely in liberalities when it should not do so much. See if you are listening to the cries of the wretched to have pity and relieve them according to your power; if you are taking care that vice is suppressed in your house and that peace reigns among your servants.

Madam, will you not say that I am too bold? You would be right to say it and to believe it, if your kindness did not remember that it entrusted me with your soul. I assure you that I am often very occupied before Our Lord with it and that in His light, I am watching for anything that might cause the least hindrance to your eternal happiness. My heart is wholly full of zeal, affection, and love for all that affects you; but even more for the things of Heaven than for the things of earth, although I am not forgetting those in my poor and unworthy prayers.

My Lady, receive from a heart that is at your feet, and which only

30. Cf. Phil 1:8.

speaks to you with profound respect, what it is interiorly con-
strained to say to you. If this displeases you, I will do it no more; but
know that your soul is more precious to me than my own, and that
it seems to me that it is mine and that I must give it to my divine
Master. Pardon me if in this I am disrespectful.

n. 99

Yesterday, you gave me a very consoling piece of news, but I cannot
take complete joy in it before I know if you had some rest tonight.
There must be some secret power which sustains you. I have no
doubt that this is Our Lord's adorable hands. My trust is in Him, for
the preservation of your very honored self. If I were to envision
what you endure, in body and mind, I would be constantly in sorrow. But you are well, you have a powerful protection. It is not necessary for a child to fear anything when he is in his father's arms.
Your soul and your entire being are surrounded by God; you are
supported by His omnipotent hand; you rest in His immensity as in
a place of safety and His sweet and gracious Providence anticipates
your needs, His grace strengthens you, and His love draws you
wholly to Himself.

It is a great joy for a soul to see itself in God in this way; to live in
Him, from Him, and for Him. This is Paradise begun; but we must
persevere in trust and fidelity, and above all, in continual thanksgiving for God's infinite bounties. We must never forget them if we do
not want to dry up their source. Madam, I know that you take great
care to give Him thanks. Let us always begin and end our prayers
with thanksgiving and they will never be fruitless. This is an infallible secret that Our Lord taught a holy soul one day in prayer.

Forgive me, I am too tiresome. You must impose silence on me if
you want me to leave you in peace.

I am eagerly awaiting your news.

n. 3091

It seems to me that you are withdrawing so much, that you no
longer want to soothe your heart by sharing in some small way the
crosses you are suffering without almost any relief. One doesn't give
up showing compassion for so many sufferings, but it is with even

89

more sorrow when one sees oneself incapable of giving you relief, because you close yourself up with your pain to hide it all alone in God's presence.

I know very well that this is heroic, and that great souls display their courage by overcoming life's afflictions, but however generous one may be by nature, the heart cannot protect itself from being wounded in a thousand different situations, and God does not forbid us to confide in another for the sake of bearing our burdens. The Son of God allowed Simon of Cyrene to carry the end of the cross, to lessen His pain a little. Indeed, I know that when God wills that a soul suffer, He suspends all the consolations in heaven and on earth, but I do not believe, Madam, that God wants you to be so destitute. It is certainly permitted you to find some aid in the counsel of a few good servants of God. My Lady, consult them and see before God if there is not some remedy for your troubles. Consider what is causing your troubles and what can be done to free you from them.

There are crosses which are in no way good to keep, and which Providence sends us without limiting the means by which we may seek relief [from them]. There are others which God's hand presses upon us so delicately and so deeply that He makes the soul unable to come out from under them. One must resign oneself to crosses such as these and, with Jesus Christ's patience, suffer and die upon their wood. The One who crucifies also secretly sustains; He knows how to put to death and bring to life at the same time.

Surrender yourself to His love's unknown plans, for He knows how to lead us into hell and draw us out of it. A soul will never perish who remains submissive to His divine operations. The hand that wounds in such dealings is both harsh and gentle, opening the wound and healing it, both wielding the sword and bringing the cure. We must not be worried in this trial; this is what divine love does in souls who, without reserve, want to be completely transformed into Jesus Christ. Such souls must be purified and, to this end, tribulations serve as fire. While in such a crucible one needs someone to help him bear it with courage, through a loving confidence in God and the surrender of one's entire self to His good pleasure. For the rest, we must let this lovable Savior act; He has no motive apart from sanctifying the soul and transforming it in His love.

However, when crosses are caused and produced by temporal things, let us take counsel and look for the remedies. If none of these succeed, let us leave everything to the divine disposition and, with unshakable faith, hope that the all-good God will infallibly put it to rights by the workings of His divine wisdom, which cannot deceive, and which acts for our good in all things, even though the human mind is not always really convinced of this.

We must not remain crushed under the weight of the things that are afflicting us. If they are turning us away from God and disturbing our interior peace, we must overcome them by a holy disdain and by withdrawing our spirit into God, leaving to Him the outcome of such hardships. Accept them meekly and lovingly, [together with] the setbacks, the humiliations, and contradictions that come of them. Until a soul is totally resigned to God in all that pleases Him, and in the manner He wills, it is altogether impossible for that soul to have a stable inward calm. May God grant, my Lady, that you possess the One whom I wish for you. The vapors would then have no power to vex you.

Place all things in God, and leave yourself there. According to His holy will, He will look after everything that affects you. Embrace this blindly, and disentangle yourself gently from all things so as to cleave to God alone. If He turns everything upside down, you must bless Him together with the holy man Job; this is how He makes saints.

God is wonderful in His works; by means of all your crosses, He is operating divinely in you; He is doing in you a work worthy of Himself and of the eternal felicity that will crown all your sufferings by changing them into joy. Does it matter what we are in this world, provided that we rejoice eternally in God?

Courage then, Madam, the end will come. All created things will return into the nothingness whence they came, and you will pass over into Jesus to rest in God forever. *Cujus regni non erit finis.* (And of His kingdom there shall be no end.)[31]

---

31. Lk 1:33; Niceno-Constantinopolitan Creed.

Pardon me for giving you the trouble of reading this scrap; it will be enough for me if it helps to relieve you for a moment. I am not worthy to serve you, even though my zeal and my affection would urge me to do more. God will supply for the rest; this I pray with all my heart. May He give you to know, Madam, what I am to you in His love, and with profound respect.

n. 569[32]

In the midst of the misfortunes that befall your Royal Highness, I am consoled to see you holding firm under God's good pleasure and becoming accustomed to the cross. My Lady, this is where the soul finds a wholly divine grace which elevates it and draws it from itself so as to bring it to God. I have always thought that the reversal of your House's affairs would serve you as a ladder to climb to Heaven. If Christians could understand the grace that God hides in sufferings, their happiness would be to suffer without interruption, for it is certain that the Son of God never gives us a cross except through an infinite love. Yet flesh and blood do not understand this language and faith is not lively enough in us to convince us of this truth. You are too much a Christian to disregard it. You must only take courage and remain close to God, so as to be strengthened by His grace, which will unfailingly raise you above everything created. Find your joy in Him, since He is all yours and His actions are filled with love and mercy. I have a tremendous desire for you to be entirely His. I am quite moved by the illness of His Highness. Age and grief do not go well together and I do not like the fainting spells he suffers. From the depths of my heart, I have prayed to God for him. I cannot help saying, without departing from respect, that I like this Prince more than I can say. He is my Sovereign, to whom I owe my life, after God. I feel myself so interiorly pressed to pray to Our Lord for his needs that I received Communion today for this purpose, in a very particular way which I cannot explain. I hope that God will grant him mercy. The most holy Virgin is his advocate and the love of the Most Blessed Sacrament will save him, I remain certain.

32. Presented according to MS Sor, 216 verso.

Madam, rest in God with this confidence. For several days I have
been wanting the honor of speaking with your Royal Highness.

n. 1461, *n.* 569[33]

What you have done me the honor to write me moves me deeply
before Our Lord: as He gave you a great birth according to nature,
He wants to give you a great perfection through His grace, making
use of the great sensitivity you have in your loss, to keep you in continual sacrifice before His Majesty. He is giving you, through this
sorrowful exercise, the means of sacrificing yourself ceaselessly and
of giving yourself to Jesus-sacrificed, through mutual love and suffering. You are on the cross constantly, and though you feel its
harshness, you do not fail to be sanctified on it. And since it gives
you the humiliation of feeling your pain, it crucifies you all the
more because it removes the satisfaction of seeing the progress you
are making in practicing the virtues.

Madam, God makes you walk following Jesus unknown, abject,
and despised, in order to sanctify your soul and preserve it from the
wickedness that the world contains, and from which persons of
your illustrious birth cannot be secure without a miracle. God, who
has chosen you for heaven, does not want the things of earth to prevent you from reaching it. Through continual troubles, He wants to
make you experience that there is only bitterness and affliction of
spirit in the possession of creatures; and that the only one who is
happy is the one who understands their vanity and deceit, so that he
is not ensnared by them; and who knows the truth of God in order
to be firmly attached and to entrust himself to it: everything passes
and there is only a moment to prepare for Eternity.

Madam, pardon me if I am so bold as to present my worthless
thoughts to you: it is with deep respect and complete embarrass-
ment. Yet since I have a very great obligation to love and honor your
Royal Highness perfectly, I cannot show it better than by assuring
you that your interests are very dear to me and that, as God desires
to make you a great saint, through trials and so on…, He is giving
me a fervent affection to pray to Him that you may be permeated

33. Presented according to MS Sor, 218.

and sustained with His grace, as with what is most precious; through it you will triumph over the whole world and possess a repose in the depth of your soul to make you unshakable in all trying events; and although I am the most unworthy of all creatures, I will present myself before God every day to ask Him for this and have prayers said and Communions received daily for all your soul's needs, for your special intentions, for N. and N.N. I cannot think about the action that God has pursued regarding the whole of this illustrious House without being deeply affected: He desires the humility of the great and that they might perceive that they rise through His supreme greatness. I hope that He will have pity on everyone and that He will be satisfied with your heart's lamentations and the prayers you are offering Him; that He will fulfill your holy desires and will crown you with an eternal reward which will cause you to reign blessedly in eternity.

This is the hope of one who will never be worthy of the humble title of your [servant]...

n. 164[34]

About our ignorance concerning God's designs [1661]

I feel deeply the new reasons for grief which you have been given. I wish that it pleased God to listen to our groans about this matter. Yet since the creature is naught but darkness and ignorance, we cannot see into the counsels of God or the reasons why He allows such painful crucifixions, except to make us adore the depth of His judgments, and the inscrutability of His thoughts. Nevertheless, these are always filled with love and mercy for souls who are entirely submissive and abandoned to Him. You know it from long experience. In His love God is trying your firmness and constancy. Why? Is it not to purify your soul more and more and to render it worthy of His love? By a thousand various misfortunes He desires to detach you from creatures, so as to lead you into His holiness. This is, in fact, the whole happiness of the soul. To find peace and quiet on earth, we must esteem only [our] eternal salvation; all the rest is nothing but bitterness and affliction of spirit.

---

34. Presented according to MS Sor, 219 verso.

Receive the sorrows of life from God. Kiss the adorable hand which fastens you to the cross, with Jesus His Son, who in this world had nothing but shame, insults, contempt, contradictions, sorrows, anguish, desertion, and death. This is the gift He makes to His elect also. From this you should realize God's designs for your soul, since He gives you so large a share in the sacred states of Jesus Christ. From these you will draw a divine strength to accept, without being shaken, the difficult events which it is impossible to avoid, knowing that we are in a world in which nothing is certain. Only the soul who is truly united to God's most holy will remains firm and consistent. Allow me to entreat you not to let yourself fall into excessive sorrow, but to act with a holy abandonment and complete trust in God's goodness.

We will increase our prayers to obtain for you the Holy Spirit's lights and the necessary graces to uphold this dear afflicted person,[35] who moves me deeply. It is this which the most unworthy of your servants can do.

n. 1398

Although you give me the hope of seeing you tomorrow, I cannot put off until that precious moment telling you the share that I take in your troubles; I would not have any comfort about them, if I did not know that it is through the path of tribulations that Our Lord desires to detach you from the earth, in order to unite you and completely transform you into Himself.

For a long time I have been trying to observe His action regarding your soul and I see that He continually causes new reversals in your affairs and expectations, although they are right. It is very uncomfortable to see oneself treated in that manner; nature feels it and grieves over seeing oneself abandoned by those who are obligated to you, according to human thinking. However, do not believe that all these events are accidents to God: these are the thorns of His crown, and thus a small portion of the pains and

35. This may be an allusion to the marriage of the Duchess's elder daughter, Marguerite Louise, to the Duke of Tuscany, Cosimo III de Medici, demanded by Louis XIV, to the great distress of the young lady.

humiliations He suffered in this world; in these you must share, if you want to become holy and imitate Jesus Christ. The small help you find in men will cause you to retreat into God, and their unfaithfulness in your regard will not allow you to trust in them any more, or to hope for any help from them. God does not want you to find any support in creatures. He is jealous of your heart; He would not possess it fully if it found a place to rest in creatures. I know there is a tremendous cost in living in a detached way, but take courage, it takes only one good stroke; you made the most important step when you gave back to God what you held most dear.

Almost nothing remains for you but to sacrifice yourself; tomorrow is the day that Jesus offers Himself to the eternal Father, it is also the same day on which He received from your fidelity the victim which you gave to Him in the person of your deceased husband.[36] I entreat you that this might be the day on which you offer your whole being to God; and if He delays placing you in the precious solitude that you desire, do not deprive Him of the repose you can give Him in yourself, through solitude and inner withdrawal, in which you can enjoy His sweet presence and enjoy an anticipatory paradise in this world. In that heavenly exchange your soul will find new life and will receive the strength to endure all the bitter and painful things that divine Providence will send. I could even assure you that your poor body would find health in it and that nothing in the world is better for relieving sorrows than joy of soul and dilation of heart.

I will have all our sisters receive Communion tomorrow for the intentions that you wish. Oh! If I was worthy to be heard, you would experience marvelous effects of grace. There is an indefinable something in me which wants to place you in the Heart of Jesus Christ. I see there such great benefits for your sanctification that I cannot prevent myself from asking God to draw you powerfully, to tear you away from yourself.

Allow me to tell you that I consider the contradictions of men as so many blows of the sword and rod which His powerful hand is giving

36. Gaston d'Orléans, Marguerite's husband, brother of Louis XIII, died on the feast of the Presentation, February 2, 1660.

you to draw you away from Court. You belong to Jesus Crucified. The coat of arms of your house being a double cross, judge if you should not be crucified to the world, and, as St. Paul says, the world crucified to you. With respect I implore you never again to hope in any creature and to raise your heart in faith toward the One who desires to be for you all in everything. Be content with God since He is content with you, and do not be troubled about anything. Every created thing is beneath a soul who loves its God; nothing can trouble it. I know that it is very harsh to see oneself without help and almost forsaken, but a person whom God is caring for and protecting is a person well cared for. Pardon my simplicity, as well as my boldness, you are too kind and you give me too much freedom; if you saw my heart you would blame it still more, and you would say that I have rights over yours. I cannot bear that your heart should fail in faithfulness to Jesus Christ's drawing; he wants to possess it completely.

I cast myself at your feet to ask a thousand humble pardons and beg you to throw this into the fire, it is an outburst of too bold an affection.

n. 72[37]

We should sacrifice to God what is dearest to us in union with His sacrifice on the altar

29 January 1664[38]

Since everyone takes pains to console you in your affliction in every way that they can, I have not thought I could succeed better than by prayer, which has continued without intermission since the last news you received. We are asking Our Lord Jesus urgently to do in you, through His grace, what creatures cannot do. And although I am deeply pained by your sorrow, I am pained even more knowing that you are ill.

Your fidelity shames me, and makes me admire the great mercies you receive from God and the generous strength with which you are accomplishing the sacrifice of the one who is dearest to you. You

37. MS P110, 295.

38. This letter appears to have been written on the occasion of the death of the second daughter of the Duchess. She had married, at the command of Louis XIV, Prince Emmanuel of Savoy. A happy marriage, but very short.

gave her to God in the first news of her reported death and you have not wanted to flatter your hopes in uncertainty about her life, preferring to remain in humble submission before God's divine majesty, rather than in the joy which could soften your pain. God wanted you not to miss a single facet of pure sacrifice. And although you are told to descend from the Cross by this vain hope, your heart's firmness was so great that you remained constant on it, without any other consolation there than holy abandonment to the divine will.

You should be truly convinced that God wants you to be absolutely His, and that He will never cease to pursue you through troubles and crosses until He is completely victorious over you. It pleases Him to possess you and to make you conformed to His Son on Calvary and in the divine Eucharist, in which love and sorrow immolate Him at every moment. Be immolated in this way, and may sorrowful love bring about your perfection. You will never be happy except in this holy disposition into which grace is leading you, and through which your soul will be raised above sensible objects.

Remember that you must render to God what belongs to God. Nothing is yours, except nothingness and sin. You are not your own, but belong entirely to Jesus Christ. Therefore it is quite right that He should do as He pleases with you and guide you through all tribulations to a blessed eternity, where you will quickly receive the reward for the great bitterness with which your life is filled. Still you must take courage, everything will pass and be reduced to nothing. It is not worthwhile to mourn about the misfortunes of this life; death carries off everything and destroys and buries us. Think only of our blessed return to God, who is our center, and in whom there is no change, but a continuance of unchangeable peace. Therefore, complete the crowning of Jesus by your patience and humble resignation, and through His love He will fill you one day with His glory. This should be your only desire as your supreme happiness. This I ask of Him for you with all my heart, being, in Him, with respect...

n. 276[39]

---

39. MS N267, 35.

Rambervillers, April 18, 1666

The share your Royal Highness takes in the interests of the glory of the Most Holy Sacrament gives me the honor of telling you some news about it, providing you with an account of what happened here, regarding my mission to come to establish our holy Institute, in our monastery.

I found all our Mothers and Sisters so well disposed and so submissive to all the rules and constitutions we profess that we find no difficulty to be resolved; and if Holy Week had not interrupted our conferences and removed our freedom to act, to finish what we had begun, we would have concluded in eight or ten days. However, being obliged to wait until the end of the Easter feast, we chose Thursday the 29th of April, in the Octave of Easter, to have the first ceremony of exposition of the Most Blessed Sacrament and to take possession of the monastery.

Each one is preparing herself to the best of her ability; it is only I who am wretched and the most contrary to Jesus's holiness, and it is a great humiliation for me. I do not forget to have prayers offered for your Royal Highness. It is for you that we will offer God the first Exposition to be done in this monastery, with all the community's Communions. My Lady, the community has all proper respect for you and complete gratitude for your excessive kindnesses.

I am here in a distant country, where I cannot get letters from Paris unless I send a messenger to Toul to bring them. This is what I will do tomorrow, being unable to bear the lack of news that I expect from your Royal Highness, whom I see always surrounded with contradictions. But courage, Madam, your sorrows will end some day and you will enjoy an eternal peace and rest. Do not cease in your holy resolution and be more than ever all Jesus's and His Holy Mother's, and I will continue to be, Madam, with a most profound respect, your Royal Highness's.

n. 1895

Rambervillers, April 1666

It will not be through these words that I will give you very humble thanks for continuing your kindness to the most unworthy of all your servants. I have too little leisure to pour out the feelings of gratitude with which my heart finds itself filled: I am keeping those for my return to your presence.

On Thursday we have the first Exposition of the Most Holy Sacrament in this monastery to introduce and establish perpetual adoration[40]: after this ceremony we will have no more to do here; we will go to Toul for the profession of two novices.[41] I would like to have already done what my commission requires so as to satisfy your wishes more diligently and come to share in the crosses that Providence is sending you daily, which I fervently wish were completely transferred to my heart, to relieve yours.

The cross is the portion of the elect; it is through it that Jesus sanctifies them. Madam, do you doubt that He has plans regarding your soul? Yes, certainly. The more I have prayers said to God for you, the more I am confirmed and inwardly certain that He desires you to be all His, and that He will not cease to crucify you until He has purified you and made you worthy of eternal union and the pure operations of His love, which is the only happiness to which you aspire. We must always take up our courage again amid the various results that grace brings about, especially since nature suffers and it is hard to live a life of suffering all the time. You must have a high esteem for God, so as to be always submissive to His actions and to have in your heart love for what He wills, especially when those actions are so crucifying. This is all that the saints could do on earth and what you try to do, Madam, in order to imitate Our Lord Jesus. I pray Him to strengthen you so that you can endure all the great and holy things God wishes to do in you.

---

40. Easter Thursday, April 29, 1666. The history of this monastery and of its aggregation to the Benedictines of Perpetual Adoration is recorded in *Catherine de Bar*, 220–31 and 304–9.

41. Francoise Charbonnier (Sr. Francis of Paola) was professed on the 15th of May, Ann Parisot (Sr. Mary of the Blessed Sacrament) on the 19th of May.

I continue to have prayers said to God for you and for the breaking of your bonds, so that you can take flight into the sweet and precious solitude for which you yearn so often, and take your rest in the cleft of the Rock, which is nothing other than the Sacred Heart of Jesus. It is there, and nowhere else, that you will enjoy a perfect repose, and that the flames of His adorable Heart will consume yours. I long fervently for that precious moment and to be at your feet, Madam, to witness your happiness, and have a little share in the crumbs that will fall from the table where you will have that delightful banquet.

While waiting for that great good, allow me to be always what your kindness has permitted me to be, with the most profound respect...

n. 123[42]

August 1666

Providence gave us a great deal of work. We almost lost our good Mother de St. J...[43] through headaches and violent vomiting. We still do not know what the consequence of her illness will be. Our Lord seems to take pleasure in purifying her by sufferings, making her a worthy victim of His love. She suffers so willingly and with so much submission to God's good pleasure that it is a consolation to see her on her bed, like a victim on its pyre, being consumed by love and suffering.

This is a joy for a daughter of the Blessed Sacrament, who spends all her life immolated with her adorable Jesus, and who lives only to die at every moment, in reparation to His most august Majesty which has been offended. Blessed is the soul who is thus sacrificed with its divine Savior, and who has no greater desire than to see itself consumed by the fire of sufferings for love of its God. You know this better than anyone, having so great a share in the cross of Jesus, and bearing it with such generous patience that it edifies everyone. Madam, this is how your soul is being sanctified and how it is advancing toward its blessed eternity.

42. MS P110, 282.
43. Probably Mother de St. Joseph.

I ask God to unceasingly increase His graces in you, and make me worthy to be, with as much fruit as zeal, and with profound respect...

n. 1913

Madam, I do not know what [trial] you have, but I sense that for some days you are suffering much more than usual, and although you desire to hide it before creatures, my soul does not fail to discern it, and my heart is suffering with you. In God's name, let us seek effective means to recover from it.

I have done nothing regarding the memoirs from the other day. We will send them to the Reverend Fathers... I am asking God to inspire them regarding your house of Nancy.[44] I do not dare to desire anything for fear of doing what Saint Francis de Sales warns against: having too many desires. With all my heart I am destroying everything my mind would want to have happen concerning this matter, so as to leave myself a prey to Our Lord's good pleasure. I ask Him to do His most holy will in all this, and to fill you with the graces that I desire for you—to be a great saint, as I desire and as God wills. The rest [of the discussion] is for tomorrow since I will have honor to see you in the afternoon. Meanwhile, I wish you a large share of the happiness of the saints and that you may be filled with an abundance of heavenly graces.

n. 1154

Around 1667

Work yesterday and today robbed me of the honor and the sweet consolation of paying you my respects and also of offering a thousand humble acts of thanksgiving for everything you did for your house and for our Institute; but especially for your zeal for the glory of the Most Holy Sacrament and perpetual adoration. Madam, you will find a wonderful reward in paradise for these good and excellent deeds. You caused the Son of God, humbled in the Eucharist, to

---

44. The monastery of Our Lady of Consolation in Nancy was aggregated to the Benedictines of Perpetual Adoration in February 1669, after two years of discussions.

102

be exalted, and He will glorify you in His blessed eternity. There is no service we render to Our Lord on earth that He does not reward a hundredfold in that life. I congratulate those who have the power to do this. I regard them as infinitely blessed. Oh, Madam, rejoice in Jesus because He desires to crown your desires and receive the glory and homage you want to procure for Him. I am eager to see everything succeed to your satisfaction. I beg you to keep me always in a little corner of your memory, to honor me with news of your health and of the quarter of an hour, if it is being done...

n. 2137[45]

Indifference toward everything created

Paris, 1667

Since you deprive us of the honor of your presence, I ask permission to bother you with these lines to know the state of your health and if the ideas against my sincerity which someone put into your mind still have some place in your thoughts.

I admit that I have had some reservation about your house in Nancy, but nothing caused this in me except the belief that Our Lord did not give you any particular insight about this. Before God I was detached about it with the resolution to not make any move concerning it, so as to better understand the commands and the will of God, and that I should wait for the answers from you. I hope that tomorrow you will learn something. I will always be ready to depart when you please. It would be the greatest good fortune that could happen to me on earth to end my life at your feet. But before enjoying that sweet and peaceful rest, your bonds must be broken. I expect you will think about this more seriously than ever. I am having prayers made to Our Lord to give you a firm resolution regarding what you should do, and after the conclusion, we will take wing to fly to our dear solitude. Make haste, Madam, Our Lord waits for you there, to fill you with the graces and sweetness of His Divine Love. This is what is dearest to your heart, and what you desire with a holy impatience.

45. MS P110, 314.

On my part, I wish for it fervently, but before we embark, I beseech you to remove from your thoughts the fault of which you wished to accuse me yesterday; it would make an obstacle to your peace and to the union of hearts that Our Lord is joining through His love and which should not be separated, either in this world or in the next, since it is in His Spirit that they are united, and for this reason they will be inseparable.

n. 2553[46]

[1668/1669]

Madam, I received the letter you were pleased to honor me with, through which I understand your heart's anguish. However, I beseech you very humbly to have courage and be certain that Our Lord, through the intercession of His Blessed Mother, will deliver you from oppression: and I have confidence that, just as you wish to exalt the Son and Mother in your house of Consolation [at Nancy], Jesus and Mary will take such care of the affairs of your Most Serene House, that you will have cause to rejoice thereby and to sing with all your heart, "*Quoniam bonus, quoniam in aeternum misericordia ejus.*"[47]

I am bidding you humbly to take up your courage again. It will not be long until we experience the strength of His arm; let us wait with confidence—and I add, in secrecy—and with certainty. Would to God that I could have an hour with you! I would tell you many things which would not distress you. While waiting to have that favor, Madam, I will tell you with respect that his Most Serene Highness, on your account, granted us what we asked of him about the omission of the title of Abbess. He agreed and took the trouble of giving me letters for Rome for this purpose.[48] It remains, then, to

---

46. MS N267, 45.

47. Psalm 135:1: For he [the Lord] is good, for his mercy endures forever.

48. On December 10, 1668, Dom Espinasse, grand vicar of the abbey of St. Germain-des-Près, gave an "obedience to Mother Mectilde to go to Lorraine for the sake of uniting the house of Our Lady of Consolation in Nancy to our Institute." On January 26, 1669, Monseigneur du Saussay, bishop of Toul, gave "obedience for the union of this monastery to our Institute." On August 12, 1670, second year of the

sign the agreement with the nuns and then we will take possession of the house, in the name of the august Mother of God, who will be the very worthy and unique abbess in perpetuity. We will have the honor to tell you more with the first postal courier.

n.749[49]

Dispositions for gaining the Jubilee Indulgence

[December 1668]

I was indeed hoping for the honor of writing to you before you directed me to do so, in order to say a little something to you about the Jubilee [indulgence].[50]

I think you understand the purity of intention with which we should endeavor to gain it, and how important it is to be truly prepared for it. In it, our soul receives marvelous effects when it is clothed with the dispositions it should have. The good Fr. de Gondran[51] wrote a little book which speaks of this suitably; if you want it, I will send it to you.

The primary effect of the Jubilee is the conversion of life. It is this that I wish to have and for which I will pray wholeheartedly. We must go from good to better; otherwise the Jubilee will be good for nothing. I know that you desire to be, without reserve, entirely God's. Let us consider in His Presence and in His light what delays and hinders us.

Small habitual sins cause us considerable harm. These are very slippery steps and sometimes lead us to greater faults. The graces of

pontificate of Clement X, a letter from the Penitentiary of Rome was sent to the Bishop of Toul to admit the nuns of Our Lady of Consolation in Nancy to the Institute of the Benedictines of Perpetual Adoration. See the Archives of the monastery of Tourcoing and the account of the aggregation of Our Lady of Consolation in Nancy to the Institute in C. de Bar: *Documents Historiques*, 259 and following.

49. MS Sor, 219.

50. Pope Clement IX granted a Jubilee indulgence to France in 1669 to ask the help of God against the Turks.

51. Some manuscripts of this letter have "the good Fr. Condren," but the list of the works of the second General of the Oratory, who wrote very little, does not make mention of this little work; thus the editors are keeping the name of Gondran.

105

the Jubilee indulgence must cut off all of this and prepare us for a holy death, since this may be the last one we will receive.

I wish that you had a second Fr. N…, he would be useful to you on this occasion. You need a confessor who with the sweetness of grace gently encourages your soul, since in the path of perfection, not to advance is to slide back, and this will happen without our noticing it if we do not have great inner vigilance. The reason is that we are surrounded by our enemies, of which the fiercest is ourselves, and this is the one of which we often have less suspicion.

I wish to lead you into Jesus's Heart, but you are more worthy to enter it than I, who am nothing but an abomination before God. However, I have some zeal for your soul and its sanctification. That is why I entreat you, with profound respect, to examine simply before God, in His light, without disturbing your soul, if you are doing what He asks of you, and if you are corresponding fully with the graces and inspirations of the Holy Spirit.

All that I desire is that you leave yourself to enter into Jesus Christ, since the Apostle's words should take effect in you. "You are dead and your life is hidden in Jesus Christ."[52] A soul who does not live that life is neither happy nor pleasing to God. It is not so difficult to live this as is imagined. A good soul like yours is earth well prepared to receive the divine impressions. It seems to me that the most difficult thing is to guard against being too human, and that God is not enough the unique goal which animates you, or the pure motive of your actions. You know Our Lord's words, "If your eye is simple, your whole body will be luminous."[53] If you consider only God in all your actions, the whole management of your soul will go well; you will be neither anxious nor in darkness. This is what can make you happy.

I implore you to be rid of a thousand perplexities of mind which do not fail to disturb you and hinder your perfection in God. I am asking Him to give you the strength to overcome yourself. I ask Him to lead you into His peace, to correctly and piously gain the Jubilee

52. Col 3:3.
53. Mt 6:22.

indulgence, and that the Holy Child Jesus may be born in you. In Him I am yours unreservedly, and with profound respect…

n. 1432

[1669][54]

You do not doubt that I am moved to the last fiber by the most recent painful event, although I do not think your House has been destroyed. Yet, however that may be, "*Levate capite vestra,*"[55] raise your mind from the earth and from creatures and see the action of God's adorable Providence with the eyes of faith.

Let us leave aside secondary causes to be united to the first ones and say in truth and with our whole hearts united to God, "My kingdom is not of this world," and henceforth it will be in the heart of Jesus Christ. It is there that you must establish your kingdom, by putting your crown at His feet. Since you have given all your domains into the hands of His holy Mother, surrendering their management entirely to her, having no longer any share in them except through her Son's spirit: and since He is not waiting until the moment of physical death (which necessarily strips us of everything) to separate you from what birth put into your possession, enter into His designs through an intimate union of your will and His. Say to Him, with a heart full of love and trusting that His good pleasure is enough for you, that you renounce all earthly kingdoms in order to be hidden in spirit in Jesus's heart; there you will win the glory of reigning peacefully, by a loving submission to His actions. He desires that His grace produce in you a completely holy use of your cross.

Further, if you cannot remedy present ills, endeavor to win the immeasurable goods you can acquire at every moment for Heaven. The more you are overwhelmed, if not vanquished, the more your good heart should be sustained by faith, saying with St. Augustine, "I will hope in God, even if He were to ruin me." Oh, if you find

54. During the Thirty Years' War, France occupied the Duchy of Lorraine until 1634 and retained it until 1661 when Charles IV was restored. In 1670 France invaded again, forcing Charles into exile. France returned the Duchy to its rightful heir only in 1697.

55. Lk 21:28. Lift up your heads, for your salvation is drawing nigh.

your sanctification through the affronts you receive from your enemies, is that not an infinite good? Do not lose the opportunity. Act before God as if everything was lost for you, so that henceforth you can say to Him, "I am happy with You alone. My kingdom is in Your Heart and Yours is in mine." Yes, if Jesus reigns in you, you reign in Him—a sweet reign that will never end. That is where you must be firmly established and where human assaults cannot disturb your constancy. Yet what a joy to reign, this glorious reign, which makes a soul unshakable in adversities! Nothing can alter its peace. The commands of God's good pleasure constitute its glory, love, and eternal happiness.

All this does not prevent you from acting when it is possible for you. Nonetheless, do everything in this union of heart and mind with God; do not allow yourself to be overcome by sadness. By means of this situation you can work wonders for your eternity, "*Dominus dedit, Dominus obstulit, sit nomen Domini benedictum.*"[56] As for me, I am not losing faith, although it appears that everything is ruined and lost. At the same time, I am filled with sorrow, knowing that, humanly speaking, you are and quite rightly so. We must redouble our prayers; we will do so gladly.

n. 3119

My Lady, I would to God that I had some words of grace, to console and strengthen you in the aguish that I know you are suffering, through these conjectures about the matters which affect your House!

God is giving your virtue extraordinary trials; but since you are accustomed to making heroic acts of love and submission to God's will, the present ills should be viewed in divine wisdom's commands, in order to make the use of them that He desires, and through all such afflictions to raise your soul to great sanctity. This is a last stroke that He is giving to your virtue to perfect it. I am not saying that all is lost; the one who wounds us can heal us. But these are crises difficult to bear, and nature gives way before them if God's hand does not support it.

56. Job 1:21.

I see you, Madam, in that adorable hand, totally abandoned to His pleasure. I beseech you never to depart from it and not to lose your soul's peace because of what anyone might say to you. You know that everything which affects you is not simply yours anymore. You gave everything to the Blessed Virgin.[57] It is for her to defend them and for you, my Lady, to remain unmoved in a full and complete trust in her goodness. You will thus triumph over all that is opposed to your peace, and as long as this lasts, rise toward heaven, where that powerful advocate will receive your prayers in her most holy Heart to render them pleasing to her Son. I cannot express to you the respectful affection which my heart feels for yours in your various trials. I do not need to be at your feet to understand them; I perceive them sufficiently by bearing them, through an

57. Here Mother Mectilde alludes to the consecration made by the duchess's brother in the following form: "Charles, by the grace of God, duke of Lorraine, Marquis, duke of Calabria, Bar, Gueldre, Marquis of Pont-à-Mousson and of Nomeny, Count of Provence, Vaudémont, Blâmont, Zulphen, Saverden, Salm, etc..., to all those who will see this present communication, greetings. Since the donation and irrevocable transfer that we have made of our Estates to the Most Holy Virgin, Mother of God, in honor of her Immaculate Conception, reserving to ourselves only the power to maintain her authority and the care of the execution of its rights, in regard to our people her subjects; we deemed that to gain the sensible effects of her special protection, we were obliged to render all our States and our peoples her tributaries; and that, as the offering of the firstfruits with which God wanted to be honored, signals that He is the principle of our goods, so too the tribute that we will give of it to the Holy Virgin should show that we regard her as the cause, after God, of their preservation, that each one knows whose we are; the protector who guards us, and the sovereign under whom we live. For these reasons, we have ordered and we order that all the peoples of our States, beginning after this, give to her each year the tribute of their goods, in their devotion; and to this effect in each place of our said States, will make unceasingly the choice of a person of probity, who gathers and receives from each family, according to the number of each, tribute to the Holy Virgin, to be used in her honor, in the decoration of her altars and images, in each one of the towns, boroughs, villages, and communities of our said States, or in any other thing concerning her honor, according to the choices and devotions of our people. We will and we please that it be unceasingly executed according to our intention, commanding all those who are under obedience to us, to contribute to the execution of this present communication, such being our good pleasure. Given at Nancy, the 22nd of January in the year 1669. Signed: Charles. The bishop of Toul granted an indulgence of forty days to all persons who will perform this tribute to Our Lady."

indefinable connection (which respect prevents me from naming), but which is felt deeply, and which I saw very specially this morning in Holy Communion. This I offered to God for you and what affects you. It seems to me I perceived your poor heart's anguish, which made me weep in the presence of my God, asking Him with all my soul's fervor, to console yours, and to quicken you with the grace of His Spirit. I am eager to be at your feet to share in your sorrows and to draw them all into my heart, which is, in Jesus, more yours than mine, Madam.

n. 2475

From Nancy, April 13, 1669

Madam, Our Lord finally has granted the desires of your royal heart regarding your monastery of [Our Lady of] Consolation: He increased the number of victims of His divine Sacrament, without depriving them of the grace that they have of being the Daughters of your Royal Highness.

On Thursday, the Son of God, in that august Sacrament, took possession of it through a solemn exposition, though it was not with the splendor I would have wished. His Highness' musicians made up for the defects of our own voices. The Most Serene Prince had the kindness to assist,[58] and this was with so much satisfaction, that he said loudly that he had not had feelings more tender or more cordial since he had entered into his domains. This truly shows the piety of his heart and his love for Jesus Christ.

Our celebration would have been perfect if your Royal Highness had been present: you should not doubt that the whole community wished for you intensely, and most especially your most unworthy servant. Our Lord did not want our joy to be perfect: He always leaves some little sorrows in the consolations of this life, even if they are holy ones, to show that there is only perfect felicity in heaven. However that may be, Madam, your zeal has produced victims for Jesus Christ and perpetual reparation for the outrages that my sins have caused Him. You will see the great good you have done in the future, Madam, and your reward will be eternal.

58. Charles IV, Duke of Lorraine, Prince regnant. Eldest brother of Marguerite.

It was time for your Royal Highness to aid the sufferings of these good Mothers, who languished and longed for the repose that they testify to possessing now with great gratitude. Madam, they owe this to your Royal Highness. They will not fail to offer you their most humble gratitude.

Madam the Duchess of Lorraine,[59] being at the exposition of the Blessed Sacrament, did us the honor of declaring at the grille that she had a great delight in our establishment in that town and in the satisfaction that your Royal Highness would take from it.

Here in summary are details of our little ceremony, which will be much more magnificent when the bigger church is in a state to use.

n. 388

How one must begin and end the year

December 1669

I cannot end the year without wishing you a happy conclusion to it and a holy renewal in His love. I entreat you to enter into the practice we have suggested this new year: that is, love and filial trust in God. He wants this of His children, and since He has purified you in the blood of His Son in the Holy Jubilee, He desires that you forget your past life so as to remember His bounties and His love alone. This is the worthiest reparation you can make for past infidelities: loving this uniquely lovable God, and entrusting yourself to His care, cleaving to His Heart and being pleased with His holy will. You should not be grieved about life's misfortunes, but having a living faith, believe that God loves you with the same love with which He loves Himself, and desires that you take your rest in Him.

I invite you to not depart from that sweet and loving trust and to be fully convinced that God desires this from you, and that without this action, you will be far from your center and from the interior peace that you enjoy so much. Love and trust are your portion for this new year. Providence gave this to me for you as your sure and easy law which will guide you safely to where you wholeheartedly desire to be. Taste a little the tenderness of God's infinite mercy. He cannot show it more clearly than in giving us His Son. This is the

---

59. Probably Louise d'Aspremont, third wife of Charles IV.

gift He is giving you as a pledge of your eternal happiness, granting you the keys of paradise in Him. Therefore, fill your heart with a holy joy and think only of loving: this is your portion; do not ask for any other.

I beg the Child Jesus to kindle in you the divine fire which He came to bring to earth, and to grant you a full measure of blessings in this new year: holiness and the perfecting of your whole self in His love. In Him, I am all yours, for time and eternity. With profound respect...

n. 1110

Part II

Meditations on Christian Life

Abbreviations

EF	*Entretiens familiers* (Informal conversations)
LB	Letters to Madame de Béthune, abbess of Beaumont-lès-Tours
LC	Letters to Marie de la Guesle, Countess of Châteauvieux
LM	Letters to the nuns of the abbey of Montmartre
LO	Letters to the Duchess of Orléans
LP	Letters to the nuns of the two monasteries in Paris
LR	Letters to the sisters in the monastery of Rouen
L Ram	Letters to the sisters in the monastery of Rambervillers
P	Paris
Wro	Archives of Wroclaw

The editorial commentary in italics is from the nuns of Rouen.

We are in God

If you are attentive to Trinitarian love
in your soul, you will have constant joy

Today is the feast of the Most Holy Trinity... What do you desire greater than God Himself who, loving Himself with an infinite love, engenders His Word, and the Father and the Word contemplating themselves in a return of delight and infinite love, knowing themselves so perfectly, they produce the third Person who is called the Holy Spirit? This is the occupation of the whole adorable Trinity throughout all eternity and it is what constitutes the occupation, felicity, and beatitude of the saints and blessed in heaven and it is the object of our faith and adoration on earth...

Every morning upon waking we should adore the Most Holy Trinity by immersing ourselves in His adorable presence; very humbly asking Him to be favorable to us and that all our actions, our words, and all our hearts' movements might be ever adoring that divine mystery. For although we do not perceive it here below except by faith, it is nevertheless a truth, my sisters, that we possess in ourselves that adorable treasure. For you know that our souls are created in honor of the most august Trinity, and that its three faculties of memory, understanding, and will are the images and living representations in us of those divine Persons. The memory is attributed to the Father, the understanding to the Son, and the will to the Holy Spirit.

n. 114, LP

I remind you that tomorrow is the feast of the august Trinity dwelling in your soul... Your task will be to be recollected ... during the day so as to adore the three divine Persons of the august and ineffable Trinity in your soul. You will adore them by saying thrice several

115

times: *Gloria Patri et Filio et Spiritui Sancto*... Live only for the love, praise, glory and adoration that you are giving unceasingly to the majesty of God three and one... and since Jesus Christ should be your glory and your praise before His heavenly Father, dwell in Him so as to praise, adore, and love Him with Him. The Holy Spirit will tell you the rest.

n. 122, LR, 1679

If you knew the depth of this mystery and the infinite love the three divine Persons have for creatures, could you live for one moment without being entirely converted to God?

You would refuse Him nothing if you applied yourself to seeing the treasure you possess in your soul: nothing other than the three divine Persons.

n. 92, L Ram

How to enter into the depths of this mystery

It is enough if we have a certain inner tendency toward God present, a profound respect in homage to His greatness, believing Him to be in you, as in fact He is; the Most Holy Trinity making His dwelling in us, the Father acting and working through His power, the Son through His wisdom, and the Holy Spirit through His goodness. Thus it is in your soul's depth that this God of majesty dwells and that you should adore Him continually. Put your hand over your heart from time to time, saying to yourself, "God is in me. He is there not only to sustain my being, as with inanimate creatures, but He is acting and working in me, and will raise me to the highest perfection if I do not put up any obstacle to his grace." Imagine that He says to you interiorly:

> I am always in you,
> remain always in me.
> Think of me and I will think of you and
> will take care of all the rest.
> Be entirely at my disposal as I am at yours.
> Live only for me.

As Scripture says, "The one who eats Me will live for Me, he will abide in Me and I in him."[1] Oh, happy are those who hear these words and adore the Father, the Son, and the Holy Spirit in truth.

n. 44, Chapter

On the evening of Holy Thursday, Jesus prayed for us to be united to Him, as he is to his Father and to the Holy Spirit

In the prayer that Jesus Christ made to His Father, He did not pray for Himself, but for the whole Church represented by the apostles, saying to Him, "My Father, that they may be one, even as you and I are one."[2] Oh, wondrous prayer! Oh, divine prayer! How could it not be effective since it is God who prays to God: "That they may be one as we are one." Observe that Jesus Christ could not make a request greater, more exalted, more extensive, or more beneficial for us.

n. 101, LB

"That they may be one as we are one." The Father is in the Son, the Son is in the Father, and the Holy Spirit is in both and the three divine Persons are but one essence. Oh, wondrous and ineffable union! "That they may be one as we are one." Through this prayer Jesus Christ asks His Father that we might be united and that through Him we enter into the union of the Father and the three divine Persons! His prayer had its effect in the person of the apostles, and as it is said in Scripture: "None of those you gave me are lost, except Judas, the son of perdition."[3] Let us pray, my sisters, and pray the whole day that the prayer which Jesus Christ made for us on behalf of the apostles take effect in us as it did in them.

n. 3157, Conference for the vigil of the Ascension, May 11, 1665

"That they may be one as we are one." Through this prayer Jesus Christ asks His Father that we might be united and that through

---

1. Jn 6:51.
2. Jn 17:21.
3. Jn 17:12.

Him we may enter into the union of the Father and the three divine Persons! Let us ask Our Lord to draw us so powerfully to where He is that we will dwell there always and never depart from it. It is there that I leave you.

n. 101, LB

Hence, we must enter into ourselves and from there pass into Jesus Christ in order to be with Him hidden in God, as St. Paul says. This will happen through the intervention of the Holy Spirit.

n. 104, LB

God in us, and we in God

Let us see and do everything in that adorable immensity in which we float like a sponge in the sea. Whatever way we turn, we are in God; we move, we live, and we breathe in Him, but it is often without thinking about it. Let us beware of continuing our little neglects and hasten to become attentive to that wondrous Presence.

Happy is the soul who has found God in herself. It is more happy than if it had conquered the whole world.

n. 2015, Maxims

God is! That is the best word that can be spoken to a soul who wants to love Him wholeheartedly.

n. 340, Conference for the feast of St. Catherine of Siena

God comes to us
to make His dwelling in us

God lives in us by faith;
He is the source of our Christian life

Ah! My sisters, if we had a lively faith in God, how happy we would
be!... God is in me! This word alone would be enough...to not
have any other occupation than this infinite treasure which we possess in the depth of our souls... The creator is in our hearts, He is
waiting for us to keep Him company!

n. 114, LP

God possesses the ground of our souls;
we must be prepared to meet Him there

There is a difference between entering into ourselves as all souls are
encouraged to do, and emptying ourselves. It is recollection that
makes us enter into our ground where God dwells. We are full of
His majesty.

n. 50, Letter

The most real and true [practice of the] presence of God is to find
God in ourselves and this is the greatest secret that thousands of
souls may never discover because they do not go about it in the correct way. I wish that the Holy Spirit would give me the understanding of this along with the ability to teach it. Let us ask Him for it,
since ultimately it is a sorry thing to possess such a treasure and not
to know it... Ah! How does it happen that we vainly seek for what
we possess in our souls?... The faith assures us that God is present
in the depth of ourselves, not only with that presence with which
He fills heaven and earth, but present in the same way as in heaven
and in our adorable Sacrament of the altar. What is important is to

119

find this secret place[1] where he dwells. Now who will teach that to us? It is faith which makes us possess this precious treasure...

Therefore, we must enter into ourselves, and from there pass into Jesus Christ so as to be hidden with Him in God, as St. Paul says. This will be through the mediation of the Holy Spirit who will give us witness of Jesus Christ, will instruct us about these truths... Jesus Christ has entered into us to transform us completely into Himself.

n. 104, LB

We are hidden in God through Jesus Christ

I was saying that it is necessary to depart from yourself, from love and esteem for yourself, and you, I am telling you to enter into your interior, remaining before God's majesty. There you will find Him. Learn from St. Augustine that all the time that he was seeking God in creatures, he did not find Him, and entering into his interior ground, he discovered that God made His dwelling in it.

n. 221, Maxims

The soul is the temple of God

Each soul has its special edifice in its interior. Yes, sisters, the soul is a temple where God makes his dwelling, and this is a dogma of faith, since God is in us more than we are in ourselves... We have a heaven in our souls, and as many souls as there are, so many are the heavens where God makes His dwelling... God makes His dwelling in the higher part of the soul... The soul in a state of grace has a treasure hidden in its ground and this treasure is nothing other than Jesus Christ. If you ask me what must be done to find Him, I will tell you, my sisters, that each one of you has a particular path by which to seek Him... which is narrow... The soul in a state of grace is already walking in Jesus Christ, and remaining faithful in following her path, will find Him infallibly if it leaves everything and itself.

n. 199, LM

1. Literally, *petit cabinet*: in the seventeenth century, a secret room where treasures were hidden.

God comes to us to make His dwelling in us

We have a dwelling for God in ourselves which very few souls enter. If I could live there, I would not worry at all about what could happen to me. You know that Our Lord said that when He was lifted up above the earth He would draw all things to Himself. Let us ask Him to draw us into the heaven that He has in us, and let us beware of resisting Him or being unfaithful. When St. Paul says that our conversation is in the heavens,[2] it is in the heavens which God has in us. St. Teresa [of Avila] said that many souls often reach a certain degree and then stay in it, not having the courage to go further, failing to die to themselves. If we have enough strength and fidelity to leave and renounce ourselves, we will arrive at that divine abode.

n. 262, LB

Our soul is the temple of the Trinity

Do you know what feast is being celebrated tomorrow? Usually in the place where a saint's relics are kept, there is a feast; people come to honor him and pray to him in the church dedicated to him.

Our soul is dedicated to the most august Trinity through baptism; it is His living Temple. It is made and created for God alone who truly resides in the soul's depths. Continual sacrifices are offered there by Jesus Christ who is the High Priest and the relics in that altar are the three divine Persons of the Most Holy Trinity. Today's feast [of the Trinity] is its dedication; it should be spent in adoration before those divine Persons and in reparation for our infidelities, for having been so often forgetful of God present in us, and for having shamefully driven Him from His temple in order to put sin there, in truth a horrible thing.

I always arrive at this: that all our ills come from our lack of faith; for, if we believed that God is present in us, as truly as in Heaven, could we be occupied with anything on earth? Oh! Certainly not. We possess the beatitude of the saints, and we do not enjoy it. Why is it that we don't live by faith?

n. 2666, Conference

---

2. Col 3:1–3.

Let us consider the interior holocaust[3] and how it must be consumed out of homage to the majesty of God within us... To be Jesus's sacrifice we must be entirely Jesus's and for Jesus... We commonly say that God is in our heart; why do we say the heart rather than another place? It is because the heart is the seat of love and of the will: and we say that the heart's depth is the most profound depth of love and the will. Yes, God is there and we must dwell there in reverence and with a great attention to God present in us. Never be without a holocaust . . . and God will inflame you with His love which will consume everything in you, until nothing at all remains.

n. 253, Letter, December 5, 1691

The "ground" spoken of in Rheno-Flemish spirituality is the place where God dwells

God has various dwellings on earth . . . and His third sanctuary is in the depths of the souls of all Christians. There is His temple and His place of repose. It is there that we should seek Him to ask Him ceaselessly to grant us entry... We should long and desire constantly to enter into that dwelling of God where His bounty is communicated to the soul in an ineffable manner... [We should long and desire] to enter into the house of God starting in this life, namely into the depth of the ground, and from there into His palace of glory where the Father, the Son, and the Holy Spirit lead us.

n. 192, Conference for Ash Wednesday

We must . . . fervently desire to see Jesus, ceaselessly entreat Him to show us the place of His dwelling... always follow after Him... and hope that in the end He will deign to cast a loving glace at us and lead us into His abode... that divine palace... He will cause us to share in His cross by inner crucifying and harsh actions which will lead us into the house of God even in this life, namely into the soul's depth, and from there we will enter the palace of glory.

n. 192, Conference for Ash Wednesday

---

3. Whole burnt offering, cf. Lev 1:1–4. In the OT it represents Christ; in us, wholehearted dedication to God.

God comes to us to make His dwelling in us

You are like [Mary] in the Lord's temple, but since you cannot always be in the church to render him your homage, you can always be in your interior where the three divine Persons dwell, and everywhere offer Him your reverence and adoration, since it is true that your souls are indeed more the temples of the Lord than material temples are. And since there is no temple without sacrifices, you should offer sacrifices to God's majesty unceasingly in the intimacy of your soul. Our Lord Jesus Christ, as eternal Priest, offers to Him the first sacrifice and sanctifies and gives merit to ours; but He desires that we sacrifice to God jointly with Him.

n. 188, Conference for Corpus Christi, 1683

Prayer composed for one of her nuns

My adorable Savior, Jesus Christ, through Your infinite mercy, show me where You make Your dwelling in me. Lead me into that secret depth, to be never again separated from You, and may I no longer be a wanderer among creatures who separate me from You by continual infidelities. For love of Yourself, grant me the grace to remain in You and to live with You, in You, through You, and for You.

(*This was accompanied by this inscription*: I ask you to say this little prayer every day, it will not be useless for you before God. I just wrote it for you.)

If you knew the Gift of God

If you knew the Gift of God![1] The gift of gifts, the ineffable gift which is Jesus Christ, who has been given to us in three ways:

1. In the Incarnation of the Word in the holy womb of the Virgin.

2. In our august Sacrament.

3. In the intimacy of our souls where this gift is infinite, real and active, although known by very few.

We must desire this gift, we must seek it, and we must possess it by faith, with humble thanksgiving and attending with all that we are to this adorable gift.

n. 79, LP

We should receive Jesus Christ with meekness
and patience; he is grafted into us through baptism

Receive the Word with meekness which is grafted into you.[2] Now what is this Word but Jesus Christ, grafted into us through holy baptism which makes us Jesus Christ Himself, just as the small graft of the cherry changes a wild trunk into its substance and makes it a cherry tree.

Our Lord Jesus Christ is grafted into us through baptism and again through Holy Communion... There is no true life except that of Jesus Christ in our souls... Let us enter into ourselves and see if Jesus is there. If it is the case, then we are another Jesus Christ. Is it His life that is animating our souls? That is forming our interior? Since it is true that He is grafted into us, like a graft He should

1. Jn 4:10.
2. Cf. Jas 1:18–25.

124

change us into His substance. Yes, it is a dogma of faith that a divine Person's substance should constitute our substance, a divine Person's life our life…

From the depth of my soul, I wish that in our whole life we would never lose this remembrance of God who is in us and intends to animate us with His life, so that we may be totally lost in Him.

n. 100, to M. de Rocquelay, May 24, 1653

Let us work to know Jesus Christ and to see only Him everywhere; but let us see Him and adore Him in ourselves. Let us remain at His feet and not leave Him for anything: He must be everything for us, since we have everything through Him.

What error not to love Jesus Christ!

n. 2427, Maxims

Nothing should hold our hearts except Jesus Christ

Preserve your interior so that it is not filled with anything except Jesus Christ and your mind should not be curious about anything, however small it might be, when God's command does not require it of you through obedience.

n. 1299, LR, 1678

The most beautiful sentence that I can give you, my very dear daughter, is to imitate Jesus Christ, to cleave to Him in every situation, and finally to tend toward becoming one and the same with Him. That is the supreme happiness of a Christian soul.

n. 1903, Maxims

Jesus Christ should become the life of our life and our only happiness

The interior life is nothing other than the interior life of Jesus Christ formed and established in a soul.

n. 1941, Maxims

Jesus Christ is all that we can expect from God's immense charity, and all that God expects and asks of us, and all that we can ask of

God. All that is contained in the immensity of His love for us is that we are gods and God's children, that we live with the life of God's children, and that we enjoy His kingdom as His children and heirs. Now all this is contained in Jesus Christ His Son.

Wro, *n.* 94

Baptized into Trinitarian love

*Through baptism we become children
of God, temples of the Spirit, and sons in the Son*

My sisters, we have a custom of encouraging you to renew every year the grace of your baptism on the august and adorable feast of the Most Holy Trinity. There are several of you who do not know the day of their baptism. There is no day more fitting than tomorrow, since you are consecrated to the Holy Trinity, and the same holds for those who know [the day of their baptism]. It is the feast of your interior: your souls being the living temples of the Most Holy Trinity. Tomorrow dedicate them and be renewed with more fervor than in past years.

n. 2311, Chapter for Trinity Sunday

Today is the feast of the Dedication. I like dedications, they remind me that our souls are consecrated to God through baptism; and every time we communicate, Jesus Christ comes to renew this consecration, and we should do so with Him.

n. 183, LR, March 2, 1680

We are consecrated to God through baptism and rededicated by the vows of religious life. Therefore, we become temples and dwellings of the living God through a double bond.

n. 32, LP

Through baptism we become God's children. God adopts us through grace, as Jesus Christ is [His Son] by nature. When we are anointed in the sacrament of baptism, if we had the use of reason [at that moment], we would hear the voice of the eternal Father who says: "I receive you as My child, as my daughter. I am placing My Son become man in you so that you might live with His life, with His Spirit, so that you may be totally hidden in Him in whom is all My delight." We are anointed with the same anointing as Jesus Christ was anointed, and that character will never be effaced.

n. 32, LP

We have great need of faith; it is given to us in baptism, as are hope and charity, but we do not exercise it. Why? These are mysteries that should make us tremble. But our senses take everything away.

Our Lord said, "The one who is baptized and who will believe will be saved." In the past this word made me rejoice, because I said, "I am baptized by the grace of God and I believe." But then I saw that I thought wrongly. My sisters, let us consider your stores. If you have faith as big as a mustard seed, that is enough. Which of you will apply it to her sister, and which of you will give of it to me? I have great need of it; I feel it, this need of faith, because if I had it, I would no longer act except in accordance with God's Spirit. Everything that could happen and that is upsetting would not be able to disrupt my peace. I would be completely divinized.

Yes, my sisters, if you had faith the size of a mustard seed, you would do ceaseless miracles. It is Jesus Christ who says this. I have said it to you many times and I repeat it: nothing is more necessary than faith. All our failures are nothing but a lack of faith. Have that and you have everything. It is a fruit of the Holy Spirit. This octave, fervently ask Him for it.

n. 2311

Reference to the theological discussions of the epoch: quietism and Jansenism

Many spiritual persons have taken pains to discover what grace is, especially because of the new opinions of the times. Some have said that it was a movement or inspiration of the Holy Spirit; but I say that grace is nothing but a participation in God, merited by Jesus Christ, grace which was not created, but made by Jesus Christ in such a way that we can say with truth that grace is a participation in Jesus Christ and that its results are the products of His love and mercy. That is why we can say that the soul in a state of grace has a treasure hidden in its ground and this treasure is nothing but Jesus Christ.

n. 2069, Conference, 1664

Extracts from letters addressed to her friend the Countess of Châteauvieux[1]

Baptism obliges us to a high perfection, which is that of Christianity, because it conforms us to Jesus's death and life, since it imprints His character and likeness on our souls, wherein all our grace and perfection consists, unlike the old law which was a law of fear and slavery. "For the law was given through Moses; grace and truth were brought by Jesus Christ."[2]

n. 1947, LC

Baptism is a consecration of souls to the Holy Trinity made by Jesus Christ. And in order to live according to your Christian obligation, you should live according to the dignity you received in baptism. ... You must regard your soul as a consecrated temple; and with this in mind, keep it pure and spotless, since it must be the sacred resting place of the divinity... God alone must reign in His temple; and if you serve creatures may it be for His pure love...

n. 996, LC

Live like Jesus Christ since through baptism you are clothed with Him.[3]... Faith is the true light of the Christian soul. It is a torch which was given to you in baptism in order to illumine your whole life, and to teach you that the knowledge and doctrine of Jesus Christ are learned through the practice of humility and simplicity.

n. 996, LC

1. For a translation of the correspondence to the Countess as she herself arranged it thematically, see *The "Breviary of Fire": Letters by Mother Mectilde of the Blessed Sacrament, Chosen and Arranged by the Countess of Châteauvieux* (Brooklyn, NY: Angelico Press, 2021).
2. Jn 1:17.
3. Rm 13:14.

Jesus Christ's eternal
Sacrifice present each day

The Sacrifice of Jesus Christ will be eternal: it was bloody on the cross, but He continues it in a wondrous manner in all souls, and He will continue it forever ineffably in the heart of His divine Father.

n. 1525, Maxims

Through the Holy Mass we have passed into Jesus Christ and He passes into us in order to communicate His divine life, to make us live God's life... We must ask Him to hide us in Himself, so that we may be reanimated, and that we may no longer live except from His Spirit, because it is the primary effect of the Holy Mass to draw us to Jesus Christ and to unite us completely with Him.

A nun asked Mother [Mectilde] how we were sacrificed with Jesus Christ; she answered, "As members united to their head."

n. 2192, EF

The Mass is so holy and so precious a thing that it would be better to lose a whole world than one Mass voluntarily; and when we cannot assist at it, we should at least turn our inner attention to it, and I am certain that those who assist with the necessary dispositions receive great graces; if one finds oneself completely helpless, one should at least have a disposition of profound humiliation. In the Mass we are presented with all the mysteries of Our Lord Jesus Christ. A soul who is a little enlightened finds there all the dispositions with which He acted and suffered during the course of His holy life.

It is an ineffable mystery in which the eternal Father receives infinite homage; in it He is loved, adored, and praised as much as He deserves and that is why we are advised to communicate often, in order to render to God, through Jesus, all we owe Him, which is impossible for us without Jesus Christ. He comes into us to accomplish the same sacrifice as that of the Holy Mass.

n. 2634

> *I exhort you, brethren, by the mercy of God,*
> *to offer your bodies as a living sacrifice,*
> *holy and agreeable to God.* (Rm 12:1)

I am taking the liberty of telling you that tomorrow is the feast of your interior, in which the three divine Persons dwell as in Their temple. At Holy Communion, remember to renew your holy vows of baptism and give thanks to God for the vocation to the Faith. I beseech you that this august feast be celebrated worthily: renew the dedication which Jesus made [of you] to the Holy Trinity. Therefore, you will observe that you are not your own, or at your own disposal, that you are God's through Jesus, and that you do not have one breath which is not consecrated to Him. Live in this spirit of faith and tend more than ever toward being detached from yourself. Hand over everything to God. Think of loving Him and He will attend to all your needs, because His desire is for you to be His unreservedly, reposing in His love.

n. 1296, LO

> *Jesus tells us in the gospel that we are by faith*
> *His mother, His brothers, His sisters; how much*
> *more is this true through Holy Communion!*

Oh, mystery of the Incarnation, perfectly completed through Communion! It was not enough to be incarnated in the womb of a most pure Virgin, You had to come to us to be reduced to nothing in us... and through this eating to transform us into Yourself in a manner so high and so sublime that all man's theology and eloquence cannot express it.

And I could say, my sisters, [this happens] in such a manner that through Holy Communion, you become the mothers of Jesus Christ, since it is an extension of the mystery of the Incarnation, and He makes His dwelling in you, even after the consumption of the Species, in a very special manner, as He Himself said in St John,

"The one who receives Me lives through Me; I dwell in him, he dwells in Me. My Father and I will make our abode with him."[1]

n. 2414a, Chapter

Jesus's love for us should fill us with immense gratitude

In all the divine and adorable mysteries that He worked, Our Lord had only two motives: first, to glorify His Father, and second, the salvation of men. Yet about the Eucharist we can say that this divine lover of our hearts is hidden there solely for love of His creature, and He will remain there until the end of the ages. Is this not overwhelming? Could He do more, my sisters? God Himself comes into the most intimate depth of our hearts. Why? In order to make us little gods and make us through His grace what He is by nature.

n. 188, Chapter, 1683

You have all received Communion and this admirable King has made His entry into you... He is a meek and gentle King... but if He is King, then where is His kingdom? It is in our hearts. There He desires to reign. His reign is a reign of peace and completely interior (all the beauty of the King's daughter is within[2])... Ask Him to rule in your hearts, since He comes only for this... The more you are faithful, the more God will remain in you and the more He will delight in you... To possess Jesus is a paradise.

n. 85, Chapter

Mother Mectilde knew the devotion to the Sacred Hearts of Jesus and Mary, following St John Eudes, before the revelations at Paray-le-monial

Our Lord Jesus Christ alone can adore God perfectly in spirit and in truth, and we can do so only in union with Him. The time when we are most united with Him is after Holy Communion. Then He draws all our being into Himself. Oh! If we could see the marvels worked in a person who receives Communion! At that time she is

1. Jn 6:56–57.
2. Ps 44:13.

entirely transformed into Jesus Christ. Jesus Christ adores God in her, and she adores God through Jesus Christ, and this adoration can continue as long as we want... You can adore God everywhere. He is in you... Retreat into God in the depths of your soul... Spread the good fragrance of Jesus Christ everywhere and lay hold of all the charity and sweetness of His Sacred Heart.

n. 261, LB

Today Pascha [Easter] comes to a close. Do you know what this expression means? It means that after completing your Passover, you must close the door of your soul and your senses so that Jesus Christ does not leave... You must believe that He is in you. Stay with Him, and do not be occupied with or worry about all the rest... May nothing be able to prevent your looking on Him... Nothing should turn you from your divine object when Pascha closes... and may you truly keep Jesus in you.

n. 1619, Conference

Oh Holy Communion, divine and ineffable, which unites us to Jesus Christ and makes us pass into Him! Let us remain there, humbled, let us be lost in Jesus Christ... and give our attention only to loving and adoring Him.

n. 183, LR

I do not say that you cannot taste this divine bread, for it has a heavenly taste and sweetness; but do not taste it with your senses, which cannot receive the delicacy of this wonderful taste. Savor it with a pure and naked faith and you will experience that it has the taste of the living God; eating in this way, you will have life in you.

The True Spirit, 1807

Adoration in
the depths of the soul

Do not fail to adore the most holy Sacrament, which is the primary and the greatest devotion and the one that all Christians should have... Accomplish this with more care and fidelity than ever, with a new fervor, passion, and love for Jesus Christ in this precious mystery.

n. 139, Chapter, August 12, 1695

Make only one act of adoration that continues always; do the same with one act of humility and try to make it continue, for if you want your adoration to be pleasing to God, it must always be accompanied by this holy virtue which will draw down to you His graces and make you worthy of divine union with Him.

n. 1010, Chapter, April 29, 1695

Let us learn to live here below like the saints in heaven, and carry out on earth the activity that we hope to do for all eternity. Let us love, let us adore, let us possess God in our souls, who constitutes the glory and happiness of the blessed.

n. 215, LO

In Jesus Christ, hidden in Him,
are the three divine Persons we adore

Every morning we should adore the Most Holy Trinity in our souls by immersing ourselves in His adorable presence.

n. 114, LP

Through Jesus Christ the Trinity receives adoration worthy of who He is.

n. 128, LR

134

Adoration in the depths of the soul

You can always be in your interior where the three divine Persons dwell and everywhere render Them your reverence and adoration.

n. 188, Conference, 1683

The adoration of Jesus in the mystery of the Eucharist is not accomplished in one moment but throughout our whole life

Our vow of adoration... has become for us an indispensable obligation to live only by the life of Jesus Christ in this divine mystery. Now, for us to fulfill it, it is not enough to do our hours of adoration: it is necessary that our heart love and adore Him always and that in all our actions we be united to Him... We should be occupied only with loving and adoring Him.

n. 183, LR

You have seen His star and have come to adore.[1] Now what should be the duration and extent of this adoration? At every moment of our life and with the whole extent of our being... Our adoration must be perpetual since the same God that we adore in the holy Eucharist is continually present to us in every place. We should adore Him in spirit and in truth: in spirit, by a holy inner recollection; in truth, by making all our actions a continual adoration through our fidelity to giving ourselves to God in all that He asks of us, because at the moment that we fail to be faithful, we cease to adore.

n. 2338, Chapter, 1694

To be adoring always it is not necessary to say: My God, I adore You. It is enough that we have a certain inner tendency toward God present, a profound reverence in homage to His greatness, believing that He is present in you—as in fact He is—the Most Holy Trinity makes His dwelling there: the Father acting by His power, the Son through His wisdom, and the Holy Spirit through His mercy. Thus, it is in the intimacy of your soul that this God of majesty resides, and there you should adore Him continually.

n. 2338, Chapter, 1694

---

1. Cf. Mt 2:2.

Even at recreation our soul should remain in adoration

You should bring a spirit of charity and esteem for all your sisters to recreation. You should regard and revere them as holy ciboria in which God dwells and takes delight. It is not necessary to go to Church to adore Him, we can do so everywhere and on every occasion by an act of faith which makes us see Him in our sisters' hearts, and this should give us love and esteem for all without exception.

n. 198, LB

Let us love God, adore Him, and praise Him unceasingly. We have only this to do and to think of.

n. 13, Maxims

Sisters, you know that there are different seasons in the year and that even though days follow each other, they are not like each other, some being hot, others cold; some beautiful and clear when we see the sun fully, which makes us feel the warmth of its lovely rays; others are dark and the air is frosty; and there are others which are foggy; it rises from the earth, so thick and dense that it prevents us from seeing the sun and feeling the warmth of its rays. But you know, my sisters, that this does not prevent it from being stable and permanent in its sphere and from continuing its course, despite all these seasonal changes and conditions.

It is the same with the sun of justice, who does not leave his dwelling in the soul's sky and does his work there during its passions, it rebellion, and when its temptations have stirred it and are making an uproar in the lower part [of the soul]. However, as this happens without the soul knowing about it, and taking no part in it, that poor soul mourns, and grieves, not knowing where to find God; it thinks that all is lost, and that it has been rejected, and so on, and this increases its sufferings, which are unthinkable.

If souls in this state had a little faith and wanted to believe me, they would remain near to Our Lord, humble and poor, waiting with great patience until that divine sun cleared away the clouds and fog which are darkening the interior. I am confident that they would soon enjoy the calm and light that the presence of God brings to the soul.

n. 2069, Maxims

As I have loved you

If faith animated us, we would see only God in our neighbor, because He is really in him and he is also His image. So let us live by faith, my sisters, so that holy charity wakes in our hearts in order to love in a holy manner in Jesus Christ.

After Holy Communion I was shown how Jesus is all charity and sweetness in that divine Sacrament. Sisters, here is our model. Our charity should be cordial, sincere; wanting and wishing for our sisters the same graces as for ourselves; embracing everyone in the bonds of charity and bearing with meekness everything which may offend us. By doing this, we will live with Jesus's life, which constitutes the saints' beatitude. You will say to me, "But one no longer suffers in that state." I answer yes, but the sufferings of those souls are not like ours, which are often caused by our passions. Those are the sufferings in the depth of the soul which do not trouble its peace in any way, and which it cherishes and prefers to all that seems desirable, since they are what renders it conformed to Jesus, who is in the soul as its life.

n. 1172, chapter

In the heart of Jesus we will receive the
love we need to love our neighbor as He commanded us

Let us try to bear humors which are contrary to us in the charity of Jesus Christ. If our sisters have weaknesses, let us ask Our Lord to strengthen them and help them to bear them. Now although they have them, these weaknesses should not remove the charity and friendship we are obliged to have for them in Jesus Christ, who bids us so often to love each other as He loved us,[1] and who makes so

---

1. Jn 15:12.

137

much of this love of neighbor that He told us in the gospel: "If you are offering your gift at the altar, and you realize that your brother has something against you, leave your gift and go to be reconciled with him."[2] Through this Jesus Christ tells us that He prefers this union and charity we should have for each other to actions that appear very holy, such as offering gifts at the altar. St. John said, "God is charity, whoever abides in charity abides in God and God abides in him."[3] Let us have this happiness, sisters, let us place this heavenly virtue very high in our hearts. It will cause us to think and act as we should towards our neighbor.

In consequence, we must renounce ourselves and the love of our own spirit so as to love only through Jesus Christ's charity. I promise you that you will become another Jesus Christ by doing this.

n. 217, Conference

Respect and the spirit of service are signs of real love

Have respect for all your sisters as for Jesus Christ, in such a way that you do whatever you may do for them in this spirit, even if it is only to pick up their handkerchief.

n. 2691a

Our Lord Jesus asked His Father, shortly before His death, that His own might be one with each other, saying, "Holy Father, may they be one as You and I are one."[4]

Oh! How this requires of us perfect charity for our brethren, and a profound union. It is the grace I ask of God the most for you, my sisters, and it is the true spirit of our Institute. I ask you to work at obtaining it always.

n. 2242a

2. Mt 5:23–24.
3. 1 Jn 4:16.
4. Jn 17:22.

As I have loved you

We must love our neighbor in truth

Love is more rigorous than the cross; it will make you suffer more…
Love truly, and you will experience what love's suffering is.

n. 112, LR, 1679

If you are held captive by the laws of divine love, you will enter into
a holy liberty which will cause you to enjoy an infinite good.

n. 2566, EF

Sincere charity requires us to die to ourselves; it is a kind of martyrdom

My sisters, Jesus Christ is passing by and invites us to follow Him to
martyrdom, but a hidden martyrdom which makes us die to ourselves, to our passions, to our bad moods, to a thousand little jeal-
ousies and rejections; a martyrdom which makes us merciless to
ourselves and completely merciful to our neighbor.

n. 1552, Chapter

I wish I could teach the true charity which comes from Jesus
Christ's heart and which we should have as members of that adorable Head, but our trouble is that we do not regard ourselves as His
members. Rather, we detach ourselves from that union in order to
live in ourselves and for ourselves as single persons. Therefore, let us
leave aside what is ours in order to remain united in the heart of
Jesus Christ, our Head.

n. 215, Chapter

I exhort you to meekness and charity toward each other, the precious virtues of Jesus Christ. You cannot receive them unless He
communicates them to you and you are communicating [in the
Eucharist] frequently! Therefore, put them into practice: live in
meekness and charity together. These virtues are so necessary to
preserve the union and the Spirit of God in us.

n. 1075, Conference

We must be only one soul and one heart—but what heart will that be? Will it be yours? Will it be mine? No, it is too abominable; it is the heart of Jesus Christ which should be our heart. You will say to me, "And why not that of the most holy Mother of God, since she is our Superior?" That is because she has only one heart with her Son, and if she were on earth and Jesus Christ in the most holy Eucharist, we would discover that her heart was united to It and not in her body.

n. 217, Chapter

A Mother's heart

Mother Mectilde is very close to her nuns in distress

I can tell you, my dearest children, that you are always so deeply precious to me that you never leave my heart, and my grief is that you are bearing crosses and that I am not present to experience and carry them with you.

n. 2018, LR, 1678

To a sister having difficulties

Come simply and confidently. Your wounds are my wounds, your sins are mine, I will mourn for you as for myself. You know that I am your Mother and that you are my dear Daughter: believe that I love you tenderly and that I am your true friend. I will hide you in my heart, I will pray to God for you; your eternal interests will be mine and I will tell Our Lord with all my heart that I do not want to go into heaven without you.

n. 432

It would be a great joy for me to come to pour out my heart into yours and to give you the occasion to pour yours into mine... Our Lord did not want it... Alas! Could you ever offend me? Never say such a thing, you are wounding my heart which loves you tenderly.

n. 414

Letter to a monastery whose founding was difficult

I am not unaware of your afflictions, nor those of your dear companions. I hope that Our Lord will grant me the grace to make you understand this, because, my dear child, I cannot tell you enough how great my affection is for all of you.

n. 1579a, LR, 1679

Allow me to justify my somewhat stern conduct to you in your grief... I am certain that if you were in my place and I was in yours, you would act as I did and you would understand how deeply I love you and how sincerely I am yours. No, once more, I am not insensitive to your pain, I know it so well that I would like to suffer all that it would please Our Lord [to inflict on me] in order to become worthy of lessening it for you... Pour your heart into that of your Mother who has more affection for you than the one who gave you life... Do not say that no one hears your sighs. Alas! I receive them in my heart in the same measure that yours is producing them. I understand your pain, I know its size and its intensity, but courage...

n. 1634

These few lines to a young superior show her completely maternal heart

I love you dearly... we must not grieve those under us, we must be a mother to all and serve them all with affection.

n. 1139, LR

In the name of God, take care of yourself! Your whole focus is to think of my health and to neglect your own, and do you not know that I cannot live without you? If you love my life so much, love your own a little more for love of Our Lord, since it is for Him alone that you and I desire to live.

n. 43, LR, 1678

I declare that I love you tenderly; I am taking tonight to write this note.

n. 432, LR

If outbursts of affection escape from my heart, I assure you that no sooner have I expressed them than at the next moment I am impressed with a holy fervor to drive the victim to the summit of the mountain where she is to be destroyed... I would prefer to die than to hinder you for a moment in the course that you must take.

Nevertheless, Our Lord does not deny me either affection or compassion of heart. I assure you that I have it, but I cannot follow it when the question is the faithfulness you owe toward the crucifying attractions of the grace given to you. Do you not know that I am acting like the mother of Meliton[1] who carried her child to martyrdom? Alas, despite my affection I am carrying you to the sacrifice, to the death and complete destruction of your whole self. It is absolutely necessary that Our Lord grant me courage and I hope that He will give it to me always and at the same time give the child a sincere confidence in her mother...

n. 2268, LB

The foundation of new
monasteries was not without difficulties

My child, beware of allowing yourself to become grieved about the delay of my return... I assure you that I am distressed about it... I am not so completely hard as is thought. I feel very deeply that I am a Mother and that you are my dear children and that I love you all very tenderly.

n. 432a, LR, August 1680

No, no, I am not indifferent to you, dearest child, I will be unshakably faithful to you, although my affection is of little use to you; but once and for all be convinced that when Our Lord connects me to a soul, it is for all time and, I hope, even for eternity.

n. 2266, LR, November 1681

---

1. Meliton, a martyr in Sebaste, Armenia in the fourth century.

God alone

Let us not think about ourselves more than if we were not in the world, in order to lose ourselves in God; not be occupied with our concerns, and not seek to know if we are making progress and what we are becoming... Our whole task is to regard God, and to have no other care than being united to Him. Here is the soul's only occupation, without any turning back or reflection... Be indifferent to whatever happens... and tranquil in any state we may be in and no matter what happens to us... The soul regards everything that comes to her as coming from God.

n. 2234a

In order to love as Jesus commands us,
we must seek God alone in everything

Your dear letters do me more good than all the direction of other people... I only ask for them from you in accordance with the command that will be given to you interiorly, because I want to learn to lose everything so as to have nothing but God alone, in the way that will please Him.

n. 1747, to Jean de Bernières, August 9, 1653

See everything in God always and everywhere, and do not be filled with what is human.

n. 1111, LR, 1678

Regard yourself in this world as a person who is in exile; everything passes and we all have to pass away. Reflect that God is the only one who is.

n. 2794

God alone

God has an infinite desire for each soul

Sometimes there are people who say, "If God knew the desire I have to please Him!" Ah! Poor child, can He be ignorant of anything? And that desire, can it be something natural in you? No, no, it comes simply from His pure mercy, it is He who is its author, and of all the good which is in you.

Be content, not with what you are, not with what you feel, but that God is, and that He will always be… The rest is not worth the trouble of thinking about… Do not worry about anything except God. All the rest is nothing.

Thus the soul knows one thing, which is that God is, and it stays there, no longer wasting time in considering or reflecting about everything that happens in it or outside of it, not paying it any attention; it remains in God always.

n. 2336a

Privation is a death from which the life of Jesus springs

In order to be united to Jesus Christ, we must be separated from ourselves, dying at every moment to all that is not Jesus Christ. For then He will conquer and reign in us.

n. 1828, Chapter to some novices

Sometimes we begin very well, but we do not get far. And this happens because we do not want to die to ourselves and give life to Jesus Christ in us. Lose yourself, my very dear sister, and be convinced that the best and highest good fortune you could have is to lose yourself and all creatures, because God will never communicate Himself fully to your soul till it has lost everything. Accustom yourself to being content with God alone, and you will see that He is infinitely sufficient to satisfy you.

n. 1645, Chapter

Happy is the soul who lives only by Him and for Him; to succeed in this, I do not think there is any other way than death.

n. 1855, to a nun of the Institute

*We should die to ourselves
so that Christ's life may grow in us*

Death to ourselves, being brought to nothing in a holy manner, is produced only by great blows, I mean in heroic acts of virtue and the renunciation of ourselves.

n. 1421, LR, 1678

The way which leads to life is narrow. All that you have to desire is the death of your will in God: all your happiness is contained in that blessed death.

n. 426

In the name of God, die, so that you may taste a little sample of the heavenly peace which all the saints have so cherished and prized.

n. 752

Let us die without delay—each one in his path, and according to God's action concerning us, which tends only to bring us to nothingness. The more we delay in dying, the more we delay the life, reign, and perfecting of Jesus Christ in us.

n. 156

May the soul be brought to nothing so as to allow Jesus Christ to rule in it with His strong and loving sovereignty.

n. 1714

The Church continues
Christ in His mysteries

One [Church] Father said that all Christians until the end of the world are a continuation of the years of Jesus Christ. This is why He comes under the appearance of bread, wanting to be food, so that being intimately united to us through Communion, we may become entirely Him.

n. 1240

The mysteries of Jesus Christ are past
as far as they are historical events, but the
Church presents them to us again each year

Let us prepare ourselves to have a share in the grace of the mystery which the Church is presenting to us. The mystery is past, I admit, and it happened only once; but the grace is not past for the souls prepared to cause Jesus Christ to be born in their hearts. He was born once in Bethlehem, and He is born every day through Communion which is an extension of the Incarnation, as the Fathers say.

n. 2573, Conference

Our Lord is incarnate again, so to speak, in all those who receive Him so that we continue and manifest Him by our good works and so that we communicate His virtues in our life. There are infinite mysteries in Holy Communion, for, my sisters, when you have Jesus Christ in your heart, Jesus Christ has you and you do not change Him into yourself, rather He is changing you into Himself. Presenting you to His Father thus, clothed with Himself, we can only be very pleasing to Him.

n. 1591, Conference

What is required to receive
this infinite gift? Desiring His coming

This is the season of desires. The Church is entirely filled with them and she shows it through the Divine Office. Let us be united to her and cry out with the righteous: *Rorate caeli desuper et nubes pluant justum.*[1]

n. 3021, Conference for Advent

Let us ask continually for the coming and abiding of Jesus Christ in our souls; not as when He was born in Bethlehem, which happened only once. Rather it is His intention to remain always, until the end of the ages, in us who are His temples.

n. 2573

It is by faith that we enter into the mystery

Every mystery contains in itself things so prodigious and so incomprehensible to the human mind that everything we find in books and everything we can say about it is much less than what it is; let human reason be silent, it is not qualified. Only faith can produce our comprehension.

n. 503, Conference

It is not a speculative faith but
practical faith that leads us to imitation of Christ

My God, how little faith we have! When will it enliven and enlighten us with its light, so that we act according the spirit and grace of the mysteries? For, sisters, it is not enough to adore and admire them. Rather, we must enter into them by imitation and imitate the virtues that Jesus Christ practiced in them. We should enter into conformity of state with Our Lord... This is how we will glorify Our Lord, by being conformed to Him in His sufferings, by having a share in His states... This is the fruit we must bring back from this

---

1. Is 45:8.

mystery... If we do not enter into them by imitating what they represent, the mysteries produce nothing in our souls.

n. 2484, Conference

We can best enter into the mysteries
by conformity and this is what is most important

The mysteries are presented to us by our holy Mother the Church for us to be conformed to them by state as much as possible. Meditate on and examine earnestly the situations found in them in order to enter into a communion of action, as Christians and members of Jesus Christ your Head; and we will never be united to Him if we do not do the same things as He did.

n. 2573, Conference

All the mysteries of Jesus Christ are contained in the most Holy Eucharist. They are always being renewed.

n. 2484, Conference

On the Epiphany

This Feast [of the Epiphany] harmonizes with us more than any other, in accordance with the spirit of our holy vocation. It destines us to adore like them [the Magi] the same Jesus Christ in the august Sacrament of the altar, which contains all the other mysteries of His holy life. This is why you can adore the Infant in His crèche with the three holy Kings.

n. 2338

For the Ascension

God renews His graces and mercies in the great feasts. That is why although the mysteries are no longer happening, and Our Lord, for example, is always in His glory, and not entering into it tomorrow [the Ascension], He continues to renew it and produce in our souls the effects and grace of the mystery in Holy Communion.

n. 3157, Conference

*All the mysteries of Jesus Christ
remain perpetually present in the Eucharist*

Since we cannot comprehend His divine mysteries let us adore them and let ourselves be reduced to nothingness. Let us allow ourselves to be astonished and lost in His holy mysteries. It is much better for us to be filled with them and possess their grace than to understand them. Let us surrender ourselves to the spirit of Jesus. No one understands Jesus Christ unless he meditates on and is nourished with His sacred mysteries, with His "states" and His virtues. The apostles did not recognize Him after the resurrection except in the breaking of the bread, and He gives Himself to us in Holy Communion under the appearance of bread.

n. 2690, Conference

*All of Jesus Christ's members
cooperate in the development of His mystical
Body in the unity and diversity of the same calling*

Jesus Christ is the head of the Church, she is His body and all the faithful should have a likeness to their Head. They should be animated by Him and draw their strength and actions from Him. Such that, Jesus Christ being our adorable Head, we should be animated by Him, sisters, acting and working only through His grace and light. And above all we should resemble Him. How is this? By bearing His states and imitating them in how we live and act. Each soul honors one of them… This is what makes the perfection and the completion of the mystical body of the Church with Jesus Christ, its Head: through the connection and union of the members with Him.

n. 2484, Conference

What makes me most want to go to heaven is to understand in depth Jesus Christ's mysteries, because here below my capacity is too limited to comprehend them and my soul's ground too impure to savor them. But in heaven a capacity to see them and taste them in God will be given to the soul.

n. 1835a

Prayer of the heart

To enter fruitfully into the mysteries of
Jesus Christ we must pray in the silence of the heart

You will perhaps ask me where God dwells in us... I answer that God is everywhere in us, that God moves us, that God cooperates in all our movements and actions more than we do. God is in us as our soul is in us. Ask where it is, and I will tell you that it is no more in your body than at the tip of your finger. Your soul was breathed into your body by God. What happens with infants is what happened with Adam in the past: Adam was a lump of earth and the breath of God animated him. That is what happens with babies in the wombs of their mothers: the breath of God animates them. God's breath is our soul.

There is a certain gaze at God which amounts to everything in the soul... to keep it focused on God alone and without seeking something other than adoring Him, and rendering Him all possible homage in silence. This keeps the soul in simplicity, elevated and attached to God for whole hours without seeking for anything other than God, and this, for God Himself.

n. 1957, Letter

And here is a little method for beginners

At the most free and convenient hour of the day, you need to shut yourself up in a little room where, kneeling down, or seated if you cannot do otherwise, by a simple act of faith in God, you believe Him to be present in your innermost soul. Believe in Him without making distinctions, believe in all His attributes and divine perfections. You can say, "My God, You are, I believe that You are what You are, and I believe myself to be a pure nothing in Your holy Presence." After these words, or others that the Holy Spirit inspires, you

151

should remain in silence, in a profound respect toward this infinite greatness, humbling yourself profoundly, leaving aside every [mental] operation, reasoning, and consideration, so as to let yourself sink into that adorable All. You must curb all the acts of your mind during this quarter of an hour, so as to feel only the Holy Spirit's delicate inspirations in your heart's depths.

n. 215, LO

As long as the bee flies over the flowers it makes neither honey nor wax. Likewise, as long as our mind is filled with multiplicities it cannot taste God or possess Him.

n. 1325, to the Countess of Rochefort

Prayer is attention to God alone, without seeking self

This is a great mercy from God and a sign that He wants you to be all His and focused on Him alone by a simple and loving gaze... He desires two things of you: interior silence, which contains in itself simple attention, and adherence to God... You must continue, whatever dryness or inability to remain in God's presence you might feel.

Do not cease to be faithful; never consider the benefit coming to you from prayer.

n. 2217, LP

God owes you nothing. If you feel rejection in prayer, if it seems to you that God scorns you, and does not listen to you, beware of murmuring as if God owed you something. On the contrary, humble yourself. Do not act like those people who, when they do not feel consolation or their little [divine] attractions, are discouraged; they mourn, as if all was lost. Those are people seeking themselves and not God.

You will say to me, "But I am distressed because I think that my aridity happens on account of my infidelities and they are a sign of Our Lord's disfavor." These reasons are nothing but pride. If it is your infidelities that have drawn this down on you, you must endure it as a penance you deserve. It is not necessary to reflect on oneself much; it is necessary to abandon oneself. Let us think only of loving Him, of pleasing Him. This is the one thing necessary; all the rest is nothing.

n. 2548, Letter

And here is a very "modern" method

When you breathe, you do two things: you draw your breath in and you exhale it out. Therefore, when you do the first, receive God into you and with the second, be immersed Him.

Prayer is not as difficult as you think. You should go to it with the intention of surrendering yourself entirely to Jesus Christ and submitting to His most holy will, consenting to everything that He pleases to give you, whether it be darkness, powerlessness, anxiety, or temptation. Humble yourself and be content with God's good pleasure.

n. 2248

Every soul is called to prayer in simplicity of heart and abandonment to God's will

One of the most intimate dispositions you could have would be to remain in His holy presence with a silence of astonishment, in that holy recollection which brings you to lovingly being reduced to nothing and faithfulness in various occurrences.

n. 3037, LP

Be faithful about remaining in God's presence without troubling about doing anything. Jesus Christ is the one who lives in you; we have only to cleave to Him in humility and simplicity of heart… Do not have any reluctance about being in God's presence without doing something, since He desires nothing of you except silence and being brought to nothingness. You will always do a great deal when you surrender and abandon yourself unreservedly to His omnipotence. Be faithful on this point; do not be discouraged about your distractions, allow them to pass and remain humbly in Jesus's presence, considering yourself unworthy of His graces.

n. 1746, Letter, May 24, 1649

Let us learn to live here below as the saints live in heaven, and practice doing on earth what we hope to do for all eternity. Let us love, adore, and possess within ourselves the same God who is the glory and happiness of the blessed.

n. 1976, LO

Solitude with Jesus Christ

*In order to pray we must
enter into silence and solitude of the heart*

What is the character of our silence? Is it conformed to that of Jesus Christ? When someone offends us or contradicts us, we cannot endure it. We have to justify ourselves. And we allow ourselves the freedom to speak on every occasion without any need. We want to see and know everything; we want to interfere in a thousand things in which there is no necessity to do so. Let us go to the Most Holy Eucharist to learn how to be silent.

n. 1193, Chapter

Silence is so necessary that without it grace would have no room to operate in a soul. Cease to speak, then, learn to keep silence and you will hear the divine voice which will give you an inconceivable joy.

n. 2567

As for me, I am learning to be silent; I am faring well. I know a little bit about my nothingness and I try to remain in it…

n. 1747

Do not go so fast; place your steps in the path of peace. Still, this does not require much noise; it requires only silence and nothingness to keep everything in tranquility.

n. 426

*We are encumbered by ourselves,
creating obstacles to the life of Jesus Christ in us*

Do not talk to me about going into the desert in order to have solitude and be separated from creatures, since I have learned that it is

155

ourselves as creatures which fill our souls with a thousand troubles and are most opposed to our solitude. I say: let us flee our self and we will find a holy solitude everywhere. We would not find this in the desert if we brought ourselves there.

n. 2231, Maxim

It is in the heart's solitude that God does His work in us

Let us be solitary with Him in our hearts. Let us never leave Him alone in us... It seems to me I cannot speak to you better about Jesus as solitary than to present to you the awful solitude He endures in the hearts of men, and so oblige you to render Him your homage and adoration.

n. 6

A soul who has solitude and loses it through her own fault must endure the penalty for it.

n. 2158

Remain in interior solitude, focused on God who is in you. Why don't you want to be completely His? This is an object quite capable of enchanting us. God in us: the Father, the Son, and the Holy Spirit. Everything that constitutes the glory and joy of the blessed is in us, and meanwhile we give it so little attention... My God, how are we spending our time?... Let us die to all that is not God in us out of reverence since God makes His dwelling there.

n. 213

The marriage which Jesus Christ wants to contract with our soul... through the adorable Eucharist... Where is the banquet of this royal wedding held? In the depths of your soul, which is a magnificent palace which the heavenly King has adorned with His wonderful treasures: His divine virtues, His gifts and mercies. There is an abundance of all the graces and merits of Jesus the Bridegroom which He gives as a gift to your soul. The witnesses of this sacred marriage: the divine Persons, the Father and the Holy Spirit. The Eternal Word, speaking to your soul, utters this mysterious word,

156

found in the Holy Scriptures: "I espouse you to me in faith."[1] This reality is so profound and so real that you never receive Communion without this sacred marriage being renewed... Prefer nothing to Jesus Christ's love, but beware of assisting at it without your wedding garment, which denotes purity of heart... or purity of intentions. Let us do everything in harmony with the divine will. This intention keeps our soul detached from all that is not God and clothes it with Jesus Christ's holy dispositions. And then it is adorned with the wedding garment and capable of being admitted to the sublime and magnificent banquet where it is filled with God. And this happens in such abundance that the soul which has partaken even once as it should, with the necessary dispositions, will never more hunger for earthly things. Oh! How well the soul who in faith consumes Jesus Christ in the sacred Host understands what I am saying. All creatures become insipid to it and it can no longer take any delight except in enjoying Jesus its Bridegroom, whom it finds "better than wine."[2]

n. 2040

Oh! It is a great secret to be alone with God and let Him do His work.

n. 684

I see that solitude is beneficial for being taught by God in the ways of the Spirit and it seems I realize this by experience, which should make me more faithful to seek it and remain in it.

There are some who say that one cannot restrain one's mind. You would be very clever, my sisters, if you could succeed in that. The mind runs ceaselessly and we should be no more surprised at this than at a bird which flies. It is said that if one puts a grain of salt on a bird's tail, it is trapped. It is the same with the mind. Let it be and only worry about keeping the heart submissive and abandoned!

n. 1055, EF

1. Hos 2:20.
2. Song 1:2.

Blessed are
the poor in heart

It is not easy to let God make us poor

Remain at peace in the midst of war; don't think too much about your poverties which will one day become eternal riches, if you know how to be content with them.

n. 598, LP

Here is what really makes for poverty in a soul: the soul makes a clean sweep of everything and strips it all away in such manner that it does not have anything, nothing at all, not even the smallest support. In the past we had a little esteem and consideration for this person; she had some friends. But poverty stripped her completely of everything... God gives Himself to such souls and constitutes their only possession. They live on earth as if only God and themselves existed.

n. 950, Conference, 1695

Poverty of heart leads us to God

We will never know what the real interior life is unless we are stripped of everything human, since God can only bestow the treasures of His grace on a heart perfectly detached from everything. Oh! How blessed you are if you perceive this or desire it, because there are souls who could become completely divine through sacred union with Jesus Christ, but waste time like children in building houses of cards, which the slightest breath of wind knocks down.

n. 495, Letter, January 3, 1680

Poverty of heart is first of all the work of the Holy Spirit

Blessed are the poor in spirit for the kingdom of heaven is theirs. Could we ever understand a truth so profound: that all the beatitude and the supreme happiness of the soul is to be made poor by the Spirit of God, to be stripped of everything, deprived of creatures, and all that they contain, which might give a little satisfaction.

Nevertheless, eternal Truth tells us that the kingdom of God, which is the possession of the august Trinity, can only be established in a soul which is poor and detached from everything.

Happy the soul who possesses that celestial beatitude, who is poor in spirit through the Spirit of God; whom grace has made poor and not the constraint of life's misfortunes. Let us love this precious poverty, let us choose it through the Holy Spirit's inspiration and say: Oh, holy poverty which makes the reign of God victorious in me, I choose you, and I want to welcome you into my heart. I want to give to Jesus the delight of seeing His kingdom there and of seeing that everything is filled with Him.

n. 1546

If you do not become like little children...

And this kingdom of God is in us, but it is known only by the one who is poor. Those who have a full heart will never possess it. It is only shown to the poor little ones who have nothing at all in themselves, whom littleness and nothingness have buried. And when everything is accomplished in such a soul, then Jesus rises like a magnificent sun in that soul's sky, which is in the depths of the spirit, and sheds His divine rays which fill the entire ground of that soul with glory, joy, love, and blessings beyond words.

n. 1546, Conference

Blessed are the
meek and humble of heart

Humility is a source of peace

The throne of Jesus is peace, but it can only be stable in a humble heart.

n. 2998

Humility does not consist of having humble thoughts but in bearing the weight of the truth, which is the depth of our extreme misery, when it pleases God to make us experience it.

n. 1700, LP

The first step that you should take is to humble yourself very profoundly and learn, not only by [intellectual] light but by experience, what you are and what you deserve.

n. 1645, Chapter

Have as many beautiful and sublime lights as you please, the most elevated and charming ideas, but if you are not humble and you are not truly mortified, then I call them all illusions. Everybody wants to be spiritual, and also have the finest spirituality, but nobody wants to take the path that leads to it. If you aspire to sublime states, then take the path to them, which is a profound humility.

n. 1932, Conference, 1672

*To despise oneself is to forget
oneself, to see oneself before God in truth*

We do not know, or we do not want to know, the secret of enchanting God's Heart. Humble yourself and despise yourself in yourself, not in words but in the depth of truth. If you do what I tell you, all

160

of heaven will swoop down on your soul and you will overflow with so many graces that you will be able to convert the whole world from them. No one knows or tastes God except "humbly."

n. 3158, LP

God wishes to fill us only with Himself and His graces, but He sees us so full of pride and self-regard—that is what prevents Him from communicating Himself. For, if a soul is not grounded in humility and contempt of self it is unable to receive God's gifts. Self-love devours them, and God is obliged to leave the soul in its poverty, darkness, and sterility so as to keep it in its nothingness, so necessary is this disposition of humility.

However willing you are to be humble, if you do not learn by your own experience what you are, you will never know yourself in depth. It is not a small matter to endure oneself; it requires great patience to wait for divine mercy's timing. It is a result of His mercy that we feel our miseries.

n. 848a

In interior humiliations let us turn to Mary

All you have to do in your present state is to bear with humility the sight of it and the feeling of being glad that the depth of malice is revealed. Up until now it was hidden from you and kept you in a secret pride, ignorant of what you are in reality and convincing you of the contrary.

In this state, present yourself to the most holy Mother of God and say from time to time the *Magnificat* in her honor in order to conquer your pride, through her humility. And in patience await the results of her mercy.

n. 2822, to one of her nuns

There are enough people who want to enter into the palace of perfection all at once, like thieves; through all that is highest and most sublime. They want to climb over the roof, but God humbles and confounds them.

n. 2479, Maxims

161

Let us find the truth of our being

Never argue with anyone; surrender in everything, always put your-self beneath everyone; think that you will never be as low as you should be…

n. 1955

If God is angry with you, humble yourself. If you are feeling His blows, place yourself still lower. If He rebukes you, put yourself lower and lower. And when you have gone as low as you should, He will come to fill you with graces and mercy, and in such profusion that you will be amazed.

n. 1214, EF, April 12, 1694

The people who go into mines seeking gold and silver always go lower and lower to find it; we must do the same to find God. Descend, always descend lower and lower into the depth of your lowliness. Go just as low as you can go; and I assure you that in that place of your misery, so low and abject, God will come to seek you and find you. Yes, He will swoop down. Even more, I tell you that He will come to court you.

n. 314, EF

Humility is a source of joy in the Holy Spirit

A soul who wants only the divine will in everything and everywhere is sad about nothing. We exhort you to a deep humility and a sacred joy in the Holy Spirit; be grounded as much as possible in the spirit of sacrifice, victimhood, and being brought to nothing, as the firm and genuine foundation of the interior life.

n. 488, Letter, December 2, 1679

Although I have known persons who are much more favored than myself, I have never envied them; on the contrary, I bless God for the mercies He has granted them, by this means taking as much of a share in it as if He had granted it to me, and through this I make their good something shared.

n. 101

Blessed are the meek and humble of heart

Humility consists in seeking oneself
in nothing so as to enter into the possession of God

If you could understand the inexpressible happiness of being nothing in everything and everywhere, you would find and enjoy a good
which is known only to the souls who desire to lose everything for
the sake of possessing God.

n. 2390, LP

We always want to be something, if not among creatures, then in
God, and nothing in the world is rarer than to find a person who is
content to be nothing in everything so that God may be everything
in her.

Everything is in God and God is for Himself. This is my whole
condition and my only joy which no one can interrupt, not even my
sins and imperfections. Hope for nothing from yourself, but for
everything from Our Lord Jesus Christ.

n. 1766

God seeks those who take the
last place and fills them with His grace

You will be more, the more you want to be less; be nothing at all and
you will be all in fullness. Remember this little lesson, it is short but
effective.

n. 2984

I ask you, sisters, what is the being brought to nothing which everyone talks about so much and which so few people know?

In order to understand it rightly, we merely have to see that God
is everything and the creature is nothing.

God is of Himself, God is through Himself, God is for Himself.
All creatures have their existence in God in such a way that if He
withdrew His support for one moment, they would cease to exist;
these are dogmas of faith which we are required to believe.

n. 1694

The perfection of the Christian life consists in becoming Jesus Christ through a complete transformation which requires the creature and all that is not Jesus Christ to be reduced to nothing. Given this, we must choose the means to arrive at that blessed state where the soul neither can nor should have any other intentions than being completely lost in her adorable center, Jesus Christ, He who alone is the perfection of the saints in heaven and on earth.

n. 1900

Blessed are the pure
in heart, they will see God

My sisters, always have this purity of intention in all your actions, do nothing for yourself, nothing from habit, but everything for God, everything for God's glory. A little fidelity to this practice will gradually make you entirely divine. Ask the most holy Mother of God to obtain this grace for you.

n. 2467

Be on your guard so that all your actions are pure and God is your only motive in everything.

n. 1955

The actions that seem to us the most indifferent and the most contemptible are the more elevated by purity of intention. In such a way that if I sleep or eat because God wills it, I glorify God more than by all other actions done without that motive.

n. 10, Conference

> *It is not our reason that is critiqued but our refusals,*
> *which oppose the simplicity of a heart given wholly to God*

You will gain infinitely when you have lost everything.

n. 1385

Always try to simplify yourself and not allow any reasoning, because if you listen to it, it will lead you into an abyss from which you will have difficulty getting out again.

n. 1383

I have always heard it said that the Christian life is a continual renunciation of everything; without this it is only a shadow and a diversion.

n. 1565, LP

We have no faith, we waste time on trifles, we are always sympathizing with ourselves, by thinking about ourselves affectionately. One word which has offended us will occupy us for a whole day.

It seems that God is obliged to grant us His graces. We want to speak when it seems good, to be distracted, to say everything we want, to mortify ourselves in nothing, and after this we want God to give us all His graces as if He owed them to us. In truth, it appears that God might be in our employ… But let us not deceive ourselves: as long as we act in this way, we should not hope for God's communications.

You will tell me that you elevate your intention in the morning. That is very good, but it is not enough, because we begin with God but we finish with ourselves.

n. 2352a, Chapter

We must forget ourselves completely if
we want to tend toward God… God makes
His dwelling only in a heart that is empty and pure

We are surprised and we ask why we belong to God so little, seeing that we give ourselves to Him so often. I say that it is because we give what is not ours. In order to give something, we must possess it, otherwise our gift is not valid. Therefore, for us to give to God in truth, we must be our own, and it happens that we never are. We say, "My God, I give myself to You," but we have already given ourselves to creatures. We are divided into a thousand pieces and after that, is it surprising that He does not accept us? In reality, to treat Him thus is mocking Him.

n. 2146

Nothing on earth can separate us from God except ourselves.

n. 2640, to a novice

Blessed are the pure in heart, they will see God

The saints filled themselves with God only inasmuch they emptied themselves of self. Alas! If we were pressed and reduced to a liquid, we would find only love of self... Will we ever leave ourselves, our own territory?... When will we forget ourselves?

n. 1075, Conference for All Saints

Mother Mectilde likes to convey
her ideas using familiar comparisons

We should always have with us a little pruning knife for cutting off this word, pruning back that thought, conquering that outburst; and little by little, without very much pain, we will begin to grow tall. It is much easier to root up and tear out a very small bush at the beginning than to wait until it has strong roots and a thick trunk...

n. 2062, Conference

You must receive everything that happens to you with equanimity, the good and the bad, the sweet and the bitter, so that you are subject to every creature for the love of God, not only to Superiors, but even more to equals and inferiors so as to be treated like the offscouring of the world... This is necessary, to the extent that your state and responsibilities permit you to be at everyone's disposal if they wish to make use of you, apart from sin. In a word, you must resolve not to think of yourself and consequently have no more concerns either about your reputation or goods or anything whatsoever.

n. 2479, Maxims

To live the Cross
in union with Jesus Christ

We need not take pains to find the Cross: we meet it almost constantly, whether within ourselves or from without. It is more difficult to exalt it than to find it, but all our happiness is contained in the Cross. It is the Cross that makes us Christians and it is the Cross that brings about our salvation. Let us never be separated from the Cross since it is so beneficial and makes us die to ourselves, to make us live in Jesus Christ.

n. 536, to a Superior, May 3, 1683

In order to bear fruit, the cross roots us in the love of God

The finding of the holy cross is a feast that happens every day, since every day we find suffering, but it is not the same with its exaltation; nothing is rarer than to see tribulation accepted and honored… How much the soul loses when she finds herself without those humiliations which are the most precious tokens of divine love!… Yet to find the grace hidden in them, we must look at them from God's point of view and receive them from His divine hand. Hanging on the cross, Our Lord considered more His Father's will than the executioners who were crucifying Him.

Remember that the cross is not found in heaven. Jesus Christ came down in order to find it here on earth, which is the place of crosses.

n. 603

The cross is your inheritance as a child of God and a Christian. If you want to understand it better, this was the inheritance which Jesus Christ received from His Father's hand.

It is impossible to be holy without the cross.

168

To live the Cross in union with Jesus Christ

Oh, precious cross, oh, most lovable cross which mortifies, vivifies, and sanctifies! Mighty cross which bears the grace to make saints, to convert sinners—in short, to perfect souls in the sacred love of Jesus Christ!

Believe me, there is nothing but good fortune in the cross.

n. 34

If I had received the Holy Spirit, I would have the gift of giving you joy by enkindling in you His wholly divine fire. Only a spark is needed to consume everything which causes Him sorrow and carry us away into God's Heart. And this, to have only a single breath and a single will with that adorable Heart, in which you should find the strength and courage which you need to endure the many blows that divine Providence discharges constantly on you, Madam. And, if He wounds you, He can heal you; and if He kills you, He will give you life. Let us have some faith and trust. If He were to swallow up and consume our whole self, we should act like St. Augustine, because our faith would become stronger. And if everything were lost without hope, then we should believe more firmly, because faith is not pure when there is some evidence; rather it is pure and naked when everything human is destroyed; and it is in virtue of and in respect to such faith in God that Our Lord does miracles. We should hope for them from His kindness, at the time when it pleases Him to work them for His glory.

Be strong and constant, Madam, through simple loving regard toward God. Wait for those moments. If you can moderate your natural activity, you will have a little peace. I wish you the fullness of peace and grace, with a perfect submission to the reign of Jesus Christ.

n. 2683, LO

169

Joy,
"always be joyful"

Joy is not a sensible contentment
but the fruit of a soul united to God

Always be content and joyful, because your sovereign happiness is
the possession of God, and nothing can prevent this except yourself.

n. 1299, LR, May 12, 1678

You are right to be convinced that the only joy for your soul is being
faithful to God. Now, where will you be [faithful] if not in the battle
against your passions and natural inclinations which are opposed to
your sanctification?... God is with you to conquer your enemies; go
full tilt to confront them boldly. Yet how will you conquer them? By
a profound humility, a holy contempt of self, and a reliance on
God's infinite goodness.

n. 3008, to a nun of Rouen, 1679

A plan for Lent

Eat and be joyful; for in order to truly serve God you need a holy
freedom of spirit which comes from a detached heart.

n. 1189, to a nun of rue Cassette, 1677[1]

We should be suspicious of sadness; it is no virtue

You know that this wretched enemy tries only to make us fall into
some excess. But sadness is his nest, where he plays his game to
make us perish, for sadness makes us incapable of true light, since it

---

1. This letter was written to a nun who was too ill to fast.

170

plunges us into terrible darkness. It makes us forget God and His saints, and renders the soul incapable of doing any good.

n. 2257, to a nun of Rouen, March 4, 1678

Each one of us must be content with our lot. We always have a reason for joy, because if there is nothing but misery in us, our contentment must be what God is in Himself. This will surely cause us to rejoice if we know how to truly forget ourselves and not consider self but God alone.

Wro, *n.* 120

A good plan for prayer

It is not lovely lights or experiences that make a good prayer, but conformity to God's will. Go to prayer in order to please God and not seek your own satisfaction... "I am here to adore You. You are infinite greatness and that is my joy; and I, extreme poverty and wretchedness, I am happy in them." Ah! It is an excellent prayer to rejoice that God is what He is...

Share in the delight that God has in Himself, adore His divine perfections, rejoice that He will always be the same for eternity.

n. 607, EF, September 29, 1694

With regard to prayer, I never consider what is more elevated or lower, but only God's attractions relating to souls, and where He is attracting them. For the simplest meditation is as good and as holy for a soul, when she is called to this, as the highest contemplation. It does not matter provided we do in prayer what God wants us to do. I will tell you that I am put into it [a state of contemplation] sometimes at the beginning of prayer, sometimes at the end. We should not fret so much. I will tell you what I would not tell everybody—in prayer we must wait for God.

n. 2067, EF, November 6, 1697

If I really believed that God is continually in me, that the Most Holy Trinity lives in me and makes His dwelling in me, the Father begetting the Son who is His Word, and that this same Word with the

171

Father produces the Holy Spirit there, that they are working in me the same wonders as in heaven, would I not be continually rejoicing and beside myself with amazement?... You may tell me that I repeat this often to you. That is true. It is because I am galled by our lack of faith, and that having such a great treasure in ourselves, we value and esteem it so little.

n. 101

To adhere to God's will

Mother Mectilde left her daughters
two words as a spiritual testament: adore and adhere

I wish that we had sufficient courage to see our misery, our falls, and our powerlessness to do all good deeds without being perturbed about it, or losing our peace, [instead] gently presenting ourselves before God who is present in us so that we may find in Him the remedy for our woes. Just as we would blame a person who, wet and dirty from head to toe, wastes time in crying and complaining at seeing himself in that state, without wanting to go close to a good fire to dry himself. Likewise, when we fall and we see our wretchedness, we fume and become anxious: namely, by complaining and becoming discouraged. This is not the remedy for our ills. We must draw near to that burning furnace of Jesus Christ's charity and await in patience the help of His grace to draw us out of our miseries. There is nothing so easy: one act of faith and abandonment does the job.

n. 1651

Let us ground our soul in the
continual presence of God through faith

We must ground ourselves in the pure faith about God's presence in us. It requires no imagination to believe this; instead simple faith is enough provided that it is continual. If it becomes deadened, we must stir it up it gently until the habit is firmly established and the soul sees itself more in God than in itself.

If we only knew the good that a soul receives from the holy effects of this presence when it is attended to in faith at every hour! The soul finds itself besieged by God even to the extent of being permeated in a way that is beyond words. Our whole trouble is that we do not want to be captive to this law of love and simple attention to God present.

n. 592, Chapter

On account of a lack of faith and trust we never experience the holy effects of this love... The soul should be entirely handed over to God; it should expect everything from His goodness; it should never be troubled about anything except pleasing Him.

It is not in the lights and splendors that faith exists, but in the precious darkness.

n. 425a

Mother Mectilde proposes the path of abandonment in faith to the Duchess of Orléans

It will be impossible for you to keep on much longer if you are going to let your trials weigh you down so. Our Lord wills that your soul should rise above all that surrounds you, and that you cleave gently to God, that you possess Him, in faith, within yourself, without searching for Him any longer, and that you be renewed in His Spirit. Your suffering nature, which, I see, has almost no vigor left, needs to make a little effort. It mustn't happen that such a splendid victim be consumed in any fire other than that of pure and divine love. That would be to fall short of God's designs regarding your soul. Your soul cannot ignore that you are being led by the gentleness and love that make one rest in God by a simple surrender of everything to His holy Providence. Abandon everything to Him, so that you stop being anxious about anything.

In matters where there is no remedy, where things are not in our power, we must surrender everything to God's mercy with a humble resignation and trust. I am certain that if we had a little more faith, we would often see miracles in our affairs, but the greatest would be the peace and the tranquility in our inner depths.

n. 215, LO

To adhere to God's will

God does not need us: His love is gratuitous.
But He needs our free consent in responding to His love

Finally, why did God want you, out of His pure love, in holy Religion, having chosen you from all eternity without needing you? So you could be with Him always, to fill you with His mercies, to bind you with a holy constraint in order to sanctify you.

Thus, it is a dogma of faith that He loved you, that He wanted you, that He chose you, that He called you, and that He predestined you, if you are not so wretched as to tear yourself from His divine Heart. For it is a dogma of faith that He brings you into that heavenly sanctuary, into that adorable furnace of His holy love, and that He wants you to be consumed by it.

n. 474

Have a perfect trust in Our Lord's goodness—I add that it must be a complete and filial trust—and you will see that He is goodness by essence.

The more God's hand presses us, the more we should trust in His goodness, since He gives to us according to our faith and He cannot refuse anything to the one who asks with humility.

Wro, *n.* 111

To live in the present moment with an
absolute trust in God is the peace of the faithful soul

I have in view only the present moment, the one which follows it I leave to God and I am careful not to be occupied with it. The reason is that I would lose not only the grace contained in the present moment, not making any use of it, but even more, I would expose myself to a thousand anxieties, difficulties, and disturbances of soul that the sight of such a quantity of affairs would cause me. And after that I would act only according to natural understanding which would be a great woe. It is not that distractions don't come to me about what I have to do, but I turn my mind from them cleverly and slip gently into God, like a person who withdraws from a great crowd. Leaving all affairs in God, I see them in Him and entrust them to Him, to govern according to His holy will. It is a great

175

secret of the interior life to act in this way, since doing otherwise we lose our peace, the grace contained in the moment we have, and in the action we are doing at that time—in short, we do nothing worthwhile.

Divine Providence is an excellent Novice Mistress which always leads to pure perfection the soul who is abandoned unreservedly to its holy action.

n. 2224

Mother Mectilde insists on abandonment,
which makes us capable of receiving the Spirit

Always see yourself as a little ball of wax in God's hand, to be formed as He pleases. Be without choice and without desire, so that you may be fit for the operations of his pure love. Do not put anything of yourself in you, but surrender yourself completely, without any reservation, without fear and without reflection, to the one who has more kindness for you than you could ever have for yourself.

n. 2933, LO

Do not ask for crosses or humiliations. Instead let us ask Our Lord to grant us the grace to accept with love, respect, and submission those that it will please Him to send us and to remain abandoned to His good pleasure.

Surrender yourself entirely, and with a complete trust in God present in you. He will take care of you; He will do everything in you and for you. He will work wonders on your behalf. Empty yourself of everything and He will fill you with Himself; He will take the place of yourself in you.

n. 50

I implore you, allow yourself to be possessed by His love by emptying yourself, remaining in reverence before God.

n. 60

To adhere to God's will

*Always be abandoned. If God allows
us to be tested, it is for the sake of giving us His life*

Rest in the sweet and loving Providence of God. Oh, how good it is to leave ourselves entirely to the care of a God who knows all our needs and what is necessary for us! If He crucifies us, He sustains us; if He strips us, He clothes us; if He gives us death, it is to fill us with life. Thus, we must remain in pure abandonment and may our contentment be nothing other than that of Jesus in everything, without considering our interests. As for me, I cannot love or desire anything but that, and it is there that I find a peace which cannot be disturbed by creatures.

n. 2648

The great obstacle for souls is that they want to do too much and they don't abandon themselves enough to Jesus Christ who alone should be acting in them.

The divine will is a kind of sacrament. Yes, it is a kind of sacrament, although it is not spoken of [in this way] in the Gospel. However, Our Lord truly intended it. We receive it often, because every time the divine will sends us some troubles, crosses, suffering, humiliation, and so on, which crucify us, this sacrament is given to us.

n. 1443, Conference for the second day of 1694

We cannot be led into the kingdom of Heaven, which is in the depth of our souls, without this delightful practice (of binding oneself to God's will) and I dare to swear to someone who desires to practice this as I intend to express it, that in a short time she will find the secret which leads to the blessed center where God dwells in her interior... A soul who allows itself to be led, to act, and to be immersed in the divine will lives from God in God Himself. The one who experiences it will understand what I mean.

n. 122

We must not take anything too much to heart for fear of disturbing our peace, but put everything back in God's hands, hoping that in

177

everything He will accomplish His most holy will, with which we should be perfectly content.

Our model for abandonment to God is Jesus

Let us remain within the order of God and adore it everywhere and in every contrary event, and never be occupied with creatures, at least voluntarily; that is our whole difficulty and obstacle. Let us consider Jesus as our model. During His holy life, He always had in view the will of God His Father. He adored it in the insults, assaults, and torments that He endured in His sacred Passion. And it is a dogma of faith to believe that the executioners who crucified Him were only the instruments He used, since it is said by a Prophet that God caused His death.[1] That is why on the cross Jesus Christ excused them saying, "My Father, forgive them, for they do not know what they do." It is true that God wants us to be perfect and we must tend toward perfection with all our strength, but the important thing is to submit and be conformed to God's designs.

We can divinize all our actions, even the most natural and indifferent, by doing them all for God and in accordance with the order of His holy will.

n. 1891

The divine will is a sacrament, it is *a sacrament containing God, and a plenitude of mysteries to the soul that understands it*

A nun said to her, "Mother, obtain for us the grace to make use of what you told us." She answered, "Ah! Make use of Jesus Christ who is in you by Holy Communion, [since by one Communion] you have much more than all I am saying to you. You have the adorable Word, the eternal and substantial Word. Ah! God giving Himself to us, dwelling within us. And if you knew in what manner God dwells in us, you would all be transported together with me."

n. 2000, EF

---

1. See Ps 39:9.

The Heart of Jesus

*Mother Mectilde was one of the
first Superiors to establish in her Institute
the feast of the Sacred Hearts of Jesus and Mary*

Oh! How pleasing a humble soul is to God. He can refuse it nothing; this virtue charms His Divine Heart, if we can speak thus; He delights in it.

n. 3003

You will have a perfect repose, through a holy union with and transformation in the Sacred Heart of Jesus; this is the blessed center of your soul, to which you have aspired for so long. This is indeed the true and essential repose.

n. 3097, LO

Someone asked her, "And the [wound] in His side?" She replied, "One can go there sometimes, but to remain there always would require very purified souls, and being very detached from self and everything created, for it is a furnace which always wants to consume. One must love with pure love, or one cannot remain there."

n. 564a

*On leaving the young foundation in
Rouen, Mother Mectilde addressed all the nuns:*

"This morning as I had difficulty in making my sacrifice in connection with you, at the moment of Holy Communion I saw that Our Lord hid you all with His work in His Sacred Heart, and I was extremely consoled at the sight of God's mercies to you. I see many graces for you provided you are faithful." The Mother Subprioress asked her the next day if she had seen them again in the Sacred

Heart after Holy Communion. She confirmed it, adding, "You are no less in that of His most holy Mother, and if I had not feared weakening you yesterday, I would have told you things that were even more consoling."

MS P101, February 28, 1678

Our Lady, Our Abbess

*On August 22, 1654, Mother Mectilde solemnly
proclaimed the Virgin Mary perpetual abbess of
each monastery of the Benedictines of Perpetual Adoration.*[1]

I can assure you that if you work at following the example of the holy Virgin you are participating in the infinite grace of her divine maternity. "What! Mother of God!" Yes, you will be little mothers of God! You will tell me that I am advancing a bold proposition here. It is true, but I have as proof Jesus Christ Himself who once said, "All those who do the will of My Father are My brothers, My sisters, and My mother…" Put yourself in a state to participate in this happiness, and ask the holy Virgin to present you to her Son for this purpose and to unite your sacrifices to His.[2]

n. 1050

I encourage you again to have frequent recourse to her in all your troubles and needs, to love her and to entrust yourself to her completely, and you will experience her kindness. I repeat to you again that she refuses her help and her protection to none of those who invoke her. Thus prepare yourself to experience this as well as the effect of her mercies. I am asking her to bless you.

n. 2467, Conference

Have recourse to her in all your needs; love her with all the tenderness and affection of your hearts, entrust yourself to her; she receives everyone and reproaches no one. Was it ever heard that

---

1. Every year on the feast of the Assumption, all the religious renew their obedience to the Mother of God.
2. His or hers; the French can be translated either way.

someone invoked the help of the most holy Virgin and was deprived of it when he asked?

Perhaps you will tell me that you don't experience it. And someone [will say], "For a long time I prayed to her but she doesn't listen to me; I don't feel the effects."

Although you do not perceive it, not being sensitive, that does not prevent it from happening and you do receive them indeed, because she has never refused anyone.

n. 2467, Conference

I remember having read in the past in the lives of the saints that one day a saint in ecstasy saw a ladder from earth which touched the heavens, and at the top of this ladder was God in all His majesty and glory. Many climbed this ladder, but when they had gone a little way up, they fell down again, and not one went up to the top: the sight of God's grandeur of which they had more understanding discouraged and frightened them, in such a way that they never hoped to be able to succeed. The saint then saw another ladder which likewise touched heaven, and at the top of it was the most holy Mother of God. Many climbed this ladder and all went up to the top without even one falling back down because, with her customary goodness and kindness, the holy Mother of God received them and already held out her arms to them even when they were so distant that she barely saw them begin to approach; through her aid and assistance they arrived at the top.

n. 2467, Conference

Let us be wholly attached to this loving Mother; let us go to her with confidence and ask her to be our advocate in this world and in the next. We never invoke her in vain when we pray to her with trust and humility.

n. 2586, Conference

I think that all the people who love the holy Virgin, who are devoted to her, should always have a contented heart and be joyful. What? I love the most holy Virgin; I know that she loves me. Should I not be transported with joy? For she loves those who love her, say the

182

Scriptures as explained by the Fathers; and when in difficult circumstances we allow ourselves to become grieved and sad instead of having recourse to the holy Virgin, we are doing her an injury. For this is a lack of confidence in her goodness or a doubting of her power, as if she were not powerful enough to help us in our afflictions or needs.

n. 175

Let us turn to her in all our needs, sisters. You say, you don't dare to present yourself and appear before God on account of the great number of your sins; His majesty causes you to tremble with fear. Go to Mary. She will purify you; she is the refuge of sinners. She will dispose the Sacred Heart of Jesus in your favor and I can say that there is no sinner, however detestable he may be from his immense sins, who will not obtain pardon if he has recourse to the blessed Virgin, for nothing is impossible for her. Her power is not limited; after God, nothing is so great. To comprehend it, it is enough to say that she is the Mother of God. Again, she has a tremendous desire for the salvation of sinners. Her sacred Heart is full of compassion for them and if you rise again after having offended God mortally, give thanks to Mary for it.

n. 175

I have only one word to say to you, which I take from St. Augustine: "Love and do what you will." I tell you, sisters: love, yes, love with an ardent love the Mother of pure love. Rejoice with her to see her so beautiful, so rich, and entirely filled with glory on this holy day of her Assumption. Do not ask me for any method to honor her and render her your homage, now that she is going to leave the earth to enjoy the glory heaven is preparing for her. Love, and love will make you assiduous about finding the means to give her proofs of your affection. I am not surprised that St. Augustine put "do all that you wish" after the word "love," since a heart driven by love is so well ordered in all its movements that it can only want or do the things that are for the beloved's glory.

n. 1067, Conference, 1663

In all your troubles go confidently to the most holy Mother of God. You know that the Institute belongs to her; she is its sovereign Abbess; all the houses belong to her. I have no part in this, you will understand the truth about that one day. Consider yourself blessed to depend on her queenship, to feel her maternal kindness and her powerful protection. You will experience marvelous effects from her help; do not fear either demons or creatures under such gracious guidance. I ask you, my dear children, to pray to her for me a great deal...

MS P 101